MINUTES 2018
CHURCH OF GOD BOOK OF DISCIPLINE, CHURCH ORDER, AND GOVERNANCE

Containing
Extant Rulings of the Church of God
International General Assemblies
1906 through 2018

Church of God
77th International General Assembly

Convening at the
Orange County Convention Center
Orlando, Florida

July 31 – August 3, 2018

FINISH
in the Spirit and Power of
PENTECOST

Daniel L. Black, Editor

CHURCH OF GOD PUBLISHING HOUSE
Cleveland, Tennessee

Church of God International Offices

2490 Keith Street N.W.

P.O. Box 2430

Cleveland, TN 37320-2430

Phone: 423-472-3361 • Fax: (423) 478-7066

churchofgod.org

A higher standard.
A higher purpose.

Church of God International Offices
accredited by
the Evangelical Council for Financial Accountability
(ECFA)

ISBN: 978-1-64288-029-8

© Copyright 2018 by Pathway Press
Cleveland, Tennessee
All Rights Reserved
Printed in the United States of America

CONTENTS

Foreword 9
Recognition of
International General Assembly Cabinet 10
Acknowledgments 11
Preface..12
Finish Declaration.............................13
Elected Officials and Ministry Leaders 14
Statistical Summary 15
References Used in This Book...................16

* * * * * * * * * *

CHURCH OF GOD BOOK OF DISCIPLINE, CHURCH ORDER, AND GOVERNANCE
(Begins page 17)

Declaration of Faith...19
Church of God Teachings..................................20
Doctrinal Commitments...................................21
Resolution Regarding Doctrinal Affirmation 23
Practical Commitments 24
Explanatory Notes..31
Resolution Relative to Principles of Holiness 34
Scriptural Principles for Ministry 35
Commission on Organization Report......................45
Celebrating Our Heritage:
Centennial Resolution (1996)............................47

Church Government—General (S1 through S20)................51
  Executive Committee Portfolio Assigments 52-56
S1. General Church 57
S2. Bylaws of the Church of God..........................59

S3.	International General Assembly	65
S4.	International General Council	66
S5.	International Executive Council	68
S6.	International Executive Committee	72
S7.	General Overseer	75
S8.	Assistant General Overseers	76
S9.	Secretary General	77
S10.	Ministry of Youth and Discipleship	78
S11.	Ministry of USA Missions	79
S12.	Ministry of World Missions	80
S13.	Procedure for Filling Vacancy of an Elected Ministry Leader	85
S14.	Ministry of Care	85
S15.	Ministerial Care, Center for	86
S16.	Chaplains Commission	87
S17.	Boards and Committees, General	88
S18.	Education, General Board	90
S19.	Lee University	91
S20.	Ministry of Publications	93

Church Government—Ministry (S21 through S31) **95**

S21.	Applicants for Ministry	96
S22.	Ordained Bishop	99
S23.	Ordained Minister	104
S24.	Exhorter	105
S25.	Female Minister	106
S26.	Minister of Music and Minister of Christian Education	106
S27.	Lay Minister Certification	107
S28.	Ministerial Reporting	108
S29.	Instructions for Ministers	109

S30. Disorderly Ministers [Ministerial Discipline] 111
S31. Offending Ministers [Ministerial Discipline] 118

Church Government—State (S32 through S45).................**125**
S32. State Overseers..126
S33. State Council 130
S34. State Board of Trustees 131
S35. State Board of Ministerial Development 133
S36. State Youth and Discipleship Board 134
S37. State Youth and Discipleship Director 134
S38. State Evangelism and Missions Director 135
S39. Evangelism Program....................................135
S40. Evangelistic Associations 135
S41. State World Missions Board............................136
S42. State Music Board 136
S43. District Overseers 137
S44. District Youth and Discipleship Director..................138
S45. Women's [Discipleship] Ministries (State)................138

Church Government—Local (S46 through S65) **139**
S46. Relationship of Local Church to
     the International General Assembly......................140
S47. Local Church Development Plan 141
S48. Members..141
S49. Membership..144
S50. Conferences 147
S51. Pastor...148
S52. Church and Pastor's Council...........................150
S53. Church Treasurer......................................152
S54. Financial System 153
S55. Church Property 156

S56. Local Board of Trustees....................................161
S57. Incorporation of Local Churches.........................162
S58. Approval of Construction, Purchase, or
 Remodeling Plans for Local Church......................164
S59. All Property Held for Church of God.....................164
S60. Affiliation With Church of God...........................164
S61. Investments and Loans...................................165
S62. Church Promotion.......................................166
S63. Women's [Discipleship] Ministries (Local Church).........166
S64. Sunday School..168
S65. Family Training Hour and/or YPE........................169

Church Government—Personnel (S66 through S73)............**171**

**(The rulings under this heading apply only
to the United States of America.)**

S66. Employment of Family Members..........................172
S67. Compensation for State Leaders..........................172
S68. Compensation for Pastors................................174
S69. Pastor's Minimum Compensation Scale.............. 175-177
S70. Compensation for Other Personnel.......................177
S71. Ministers' Retirement Plan
 Church of God Benefits Board, Inc. 178
S72. Aged Ministers' Pensioning Plan.........................182
S73. Insurance..183

**Business Session
Church of God**

77th International General Assembly **185**

Financial Report (Fiscal Years 2016-17 and 2017-18) **211**

INDEX **223**

FOREWORD

The Church of God is pleased to present this 2018 edition of the book of *Minutes*, the *Church of God Book of Discipline, Church Order, and Governance*. The General Secretary of the Church of God, by virtue of his office, and the responsibilities of his office, is required to make available to the church, the book of *Minutes*, following each biennial International General Assembly of the Church of God.

This book of *Minutes* contains: a compilation of all rulings of Church of God General Assemblies from 1906 to 2018 that are still in effect (pages 17-183); an account of the business of the church conducted by the 2018 General Assembly (pages 185-210); and a financial report of the receipts and expenditures of the Church of God International Offices (pages 211-222). There is also a thorough Table of Contents at the front of the book, and a thorough Index at the end of the book.

The book of *Minutes* is in continual use by general church leaders, state and regional overseers, missionaries, educators, pastors, church treasurers, and church members. Outside the church, the book of *Minutes* is consulted by judges, attorneys, and bankers, for whom it is a legal document.

Pages 19 through 49 of the book of *Minutes* are a Scriptural setting forth of the official positions of the Church of God regarding doctrine and practical Christian living. Reading and studying this portion of the book of *Minutes* can be beneficial to new converts seeking to learn about the Church of God, as well as to seasoned church members, pastors, and church leaders who wish to inform and remind themselves of the doctrinal and practical stances of the Church of God.

The 2018 General Assembly limited state directors of Youth and Discipleship to a tenure of four years in any one state or region; allowed field directors' offices in countries outside the United States and Canada to issue credentials for the first two levels of ministry; provided for pastors to have sabbaticals; required newly appointed state overseers to have at least five years of pastoral experience; increased the recommended contribution of the local church to the Church of God Ministers' Retirement Plan for the pastor from five percent to ten percent of the amount of his/her cash compensation; and called for the creation of several task forces to bring reports and recommendations to the 2020 General Council/General Assembly to keep the church focused on the FINISH Commitment. (See the **Preface** and the **Finish Declaration**, pages 12-13.)

John D. Childers
Church of God Secretary General

Special Recognition

The International General Assembly Cabinet deserves our thanks for all of the long hours and hard work they put in to make the 77th International General Assembly operate smoothly and successfully.

International General Assembly Cabinet

Presiding Bishop *Timothy M. Hill*
Executive Bishop *John D. Childers*, Chairman

David W. Ray	*Kevin D. Brooks*
Art Rhodes	*Raymond D. Hodge*
David C. Blair	*Anthony T. Pelt*
H. W. Dusty Wilson, Jr.	*Yvette Santana*
Kenneth R. Bell	*Dennis Watkins*

ACKNOWLEDGMENTS

This publication of the book of *Minutes* of the 77th International General Assembly of the Church of God is presented with grateful appreciation to the following.

INTERNATIONAL GENERAL ASSEMBLY *MINUTES* COMMITTEE
John D. Childers, Liaison to the Executive Committee, Chairman
H. W. Dusty Wilson, Jr., Co-Chairman   *Raymond D. Hodge*
David W. Ray   *Michael L. Baker*
Daniel L. Black   *Denise S. Watkins*

INTERNATIONAL EXECUTIVE COMMITTEE STAFF, 2018 GENERAL ASSEMBLY
Belinda Sherlin, Executive Assistant to the General Overseer
Virgie Parker, Executive Assistant to the First Assistant General Overseer
Veva Rose, Executive Assistant to the Second Assistant General Overseer
Robin Cole, Executive Assistant to the Third Assistant General Overseer
Denise S. Watkins, Executive Assistant to the Secretary General
Leslie Thacker, Executive Assistant to the Secretary General
Sandy Whitmire, Administrative Secretary to the Administrative Liaison
Toika Sherlin, Executive Assistant
Susana Gongora, Executive Assistant

CHURCH OF GOD PUBLISHING HOUSE
David W. Ray, Director of Publications
Lance Colkmire, Managing Editor
Elaine McDavid, Secretary to the Managing Editor
Daniel L. Black, Editor, book of *Minutes* 2018
Tammy J. Hatfield, Editorial Assistant
Michael McDonald, Cover Design
Shelia Stewart, Typesetting and Graphic Design

PREFACE

The *Church of God Book of Discipline, Church Order, and Governance*, simply called by most the *Minutes*, is the official book of guidance and polity for the Church of God, Cleveland, Tennessee. The book of *Minutes* includes information on doctrine and practices, provides guidance and governance for the church at the local, state, and international levels, contains policies and direction for ministers and other church-related personnel, and contains the official record of business conducted by the 77th Church of God International General Assembly.

Since the General Assembly meets only in even-numbered years, it serves as a launching pad for the "theme" and focus of the church for the ensuing two-year period. At the 2016 International General Assembly, the church launched the "FINISH Commitment" initiative that has inspired and led our movement the past two years, as we work together toward finishing the Great Commission (Matthew 28:19-20). In continuing this focus, the theme for the 77th Church of God International General Assembly was *"FINISH in the Spirit and Power of Pentecost."*

Meeting again in Orlando, Florida, a favorite location for the General Assembly, the heat on the outside was equaled by the heat and fervor of the Word of God inside, as the Spirit and power of Pentecost fell on delegates assembled in the Orange County Convention Center.

During the General Council sessions, special orders for each day were led by Dr. Mark Rutland, Rev. Bruce Deel, and Pastor Samuel Rodriguez, addressing the application of the FINISH Commitment in the context of the minister's personal journey, urban transformation, and national revival, respectively. During these special times, the Spirit and power of Pentecost were evident as we worshiped and prayed together.

Due to changes in the tenures of general church leaders that became effective in 2012 and 2016, the only election of leaders held at this Assembly was for the Council of Eighteen, with all other elected leaders continuing to serve until 2020. This made more time available for conducting the business of the International General Council of ordained bishops.

While much important business was conducted by the 77th Church of God International General Council and General Assembly, this Assembly will be remembered most for the Spirit-filled worship services, and Spirit-anointed singing and preaching each evening. All in attendance were encouraged to "Go . . . and make disciples of all the nations, baptizing them in the name of the Father and of the Son and the Holy Spirit," and to "FINISH" the Great Commission "in the Spirit and Power of Pentecost." (See the **Finish Declaration** on the facing page.)

Timothy M. Hill
Church of God General Overseer

FINISH DECLARATION

WHEREAS, as a part of the Body of Christ, representing different cultures, ethnicities, and regions of the world, we come together as this body, the Church of God, to make the following commitments to fulfill and FINISH the Great Commission; and

WHEREAS, we commit to FIND the unengaged and unreached people groups around the world and tell them of the saving grace of our Lord and Savior, Jesus Christ. We will use our denominational platform for cultural understanding, missional strategies, Bible translation, evangelism, church planting, and discipleship. Joining with other like believers, we will strive to have the Bible translated into every language and a missionary presence in the remaining 3,000 unreached people groups of the world; and

WHEREAS, we commit to INTERCEDE for harmony throughout the Body of Christ, humility before Christ, healing of the sick, and for a harvest of the lost. We will earnestly study God's Word and pray that His Word becomes life in us. We will pray to know our part in God's heart and our role in God's work. We will ask the Lord to send a sweeping, life-giving and life-changing revival to this sin-darkened world; and

WHEREAS, we commit to NETWORK among ourselves and with other believers for the synergizing and mobilizing of the entire Body of Christ toward the fulfillment of the Great Commission. Even though we may come from different backgrounds, different nations, and different cultures, we recognize that we are all covered under the same salvation. We pledge to not allow any differences to stop us from working together to have a global impact for the Kingdom of God; and

WHEREAS, we commit to INVEST our time, thoughts, talents, churches and treasures into reaching the unengaged and unreached people groups of the world with the Good News of Jesus Christ. We choose not to duplicate the efforts of our fellow-laborers, but to spend our God-given resources wisely. We will encourage Christ-followers everywhere to move from criticizing to complimenting, from complaining to connecting, and from competing to completing the Great Commission together. We will not care who gets the credit as long as God gets the glory; and

WHEREAS, we commit to SEND ministers and missionaries not only into regions where the Gospel is not, but also into regions where the Gospel is, in order to consistently move toward the FINISH line. We will measure a church's success, not by its seating capacity, but by its sending capacity. We agree that every area of the globe must send ministers of the Gospel into the harvest fields, if we are going to reach the entire world, recognizing that the mission field must become a mission force; and WHEREAS, we commit to HARVEST lost souls until every person has heard of the saving grace of our Lord and Savior, Jesus Christ. We will motivate and train our leaders to FINISH the Great Commission, and we will mobilize and equip our churches to grow and go into every corner of the earth;

NOW THEREFORE BE IT RESOLVED, that the Church of God, individually and collectively, sets as our vision and goal to fulfill and FINISH the Great Commission, believing that with God's help and guidance, this will be accomplished.

ELECTED INTERNATIONAL OFFICIALS AND MINISTRY LEADERS

CHURCH OF GOD
INTERNATIONAL EXECUTIVE COUNCIL

(The International Executive Committee, with the Council of Eighteen, comprise the International Executive Council of the Church of God.)

International Executive Committee (2016-20)

General Overseer	Timothy Mark Hill
First Assistant General Overseer	Raymond F. Culpepper
Second Assistant General Overseer	J. David Stephens
Third Assistant General Overseer	David E. Ramírez S.
Secretary General	John D. Childers

Council of Eighteen (2018-20)

Mark L. Williams	*Travis C. Johnson*
Gary J. Lewis	*Eliezer Bonilla*
H. Loran Livingston	*Thomas A. Madden*
Ishmael Prince Charles	*Niko Njotorahardjo*
Kevin M. McGlamery	*Barry A. Clardy*
Sean Stewart O'Neal	*Keith L. Ivester*
Gerald E. McGinnis	*Jerry D. Madden*
Timothy Wayne Oldfield	*T. Wayne Dority*
T. Bryan Cutshall	*Terry R. Hart*

Ex Officio Members: moderator of the Full Gospel Church of God in South Africa, and the Overseer of the Church of God in Indonesia

Appointed by the Executive Committee:

H. W. Dusty Wilson, Jr., Administrative Liaison to the General Overseer

Dee Raff, Special Assistant to the General Overseer

MINISTRY OF YOUTH AND DISCIPLESHIP (2016-20)

Director	David C. Blair
Assistant Director	Rob Bailey

MINISTRY OF WORLD MISSIONS (2016-20)

Director	David M. Griffis
Assistant Director	M. Thomas Propes

STATISTICAL SUMMARY
AUGUST 2016-2018

	2016	2018
CHURCHES		
United States of America	6,443	6,429
Canada	149	145
World Missions	31,710	32,415
WORLD TOTAL CHURCHES	38,302	38,989
MEMBERSHIP		
United States of America	1,158,686	1,181,109
Canada	17,463	17,998
World Missions	6,197,836	6,317,851
WORLD TOTAL MEMBERSHIP	7,373,985	7,516,958
MINISTERS		
Ordained Bishops	12,463	12,870
Ordained Ministers	11,144	11,717
Exhorters	18,781	19,878
Music and C.E. Ministers	329	326
TOTAL MINISTERS	42,717	44,791

REFERENCES USED IN THIS BOOK

The capital letter S followed by an Arabic numeral (**S20** or **S46**, for example) identifies all major headings (Sections) in **this book**.

Under major headings identified by an S number:

Roman numerals identify subheadings.
Capital letters identify divisions under subheadings.
Arabic numerals identify paragraphs or numbered sections within a division.

Capital letter A as in (58th A., 1980,) means 58th General Assembly, 1980.

DF as in (DF 4) means Declaration of Faith, Article 4.

CT as in (CT 6) means Church Teaching, Number 6.

Bk.M. means *Book of Minutes* (1906-1917).

LAMA as in (LAMA) means *Like a Mighty Army, A History of the Church of God, Definitive Edition (1996)*—the Church of God history by Dr. Charles W. Conn.

In the references, **a year listed in brackets,** such as [1994], indicates some action taken by the International Executive Council or the International Executive Committee.

In the references, **numbers in parentheses**, such as (14) or (8), mean Item 14 or Item 8.

Words in brackets [ ] indicate an editorial correction or explanation.

State Overseer as used herein may refer to the overseer of a state, states, or part of a state in the U.S.A., or to the overseer of a designated country, region or territory. Terms used may be *state overseer, state/territorial overseer,* or *state/regional overseer.*

The terms *Biblical* and *Scriptural*, as used in this book, mean, based on or consistent with the teachings of the 66 books of the Protestant Bible, Old and New Testaments.

CHURCH OF GOD BOOK OF DISCIPLINE, CHURCH ORDER, AND GOVERNANCE

DECLARATION OF FAITH

CHURCH TEACHINGS

CHURCH GOVERNMENT—GENERAL

CHURCH GOVERNMENT—MINISTRY

CHURCH GOVERNMENT—STATE

CHURCH GOVERNMENT—LOCAL

CHURCH GOVERNMENT—PERSONNEL
(This Heading Only for USA)

DECLARATION OF FAITH (42nd A., 1948, pp. 31, 32)
We believe
1. In the verbal inspiration of the Bible.
2. In one God eternally existing in three persons; namely, the Father, Son, and Holy Ghost.
3. That Jesus Christ is the only begotten Son of the Father, conceived of the Holy Ghost, and born of the Virgin Mary. That Jesus was crucified, buried, and raised from the dead. That He ascended to heaven and is today at the right hand of the Father as the Intercessor.
4. That all have sinned and come short of the glory of God and that repentance is commanded of God for all and necessary for forgiveness of sins.
5. That justification, regeneration, and the new birth are wrought by faith in the blood of Jesus Christ.
6. In sanctification subsequent to the new birth, through faith in the blood of Christ; through the Word, and by the Holy Ghost.
7. Holiness to be God's standard of living for His people.
8. In the baptism with the Holy Ghost subsequent to a clean heart.
9. In speaking with other tongues as the Spirit gives utterance and that it is the initial evidence of the baptism in the Holy Ghost.
10. In water baptism by immersion, and all who repent should be baptized in the name of the Father, and of the Son, and of the Holy Ghost.
11. Divine healing is provided for all in the Atonement.
12. In the Lord's Supper and washing of the saints' feet.
13. In the premillennial second coming of Jesus. First, to resurrect the righteous dead and to catch away the living saints to Him in the air. Second, to reign on the earth a thousand years.
14. In the bodily resurrection; eternal life for the righteous, and eternal punishment for the wicked.

Loyalty to Statements of Faith
We recommend that the president, board of directors, and faculty members of Lee University and all other Church of God schools, sign a contract that they will not teach, publish, or allow to be taught or published anything contrary to the Declaration of Faith,

or any other established doctrine of the church (43rd A., 1950, p. 16; 54th A., 1972, p. 55).

Posting Declaration of Faith

We further recommend that a copy of the Declaration of Faith be posted in the offices of the general overseer, the general director of Publications, and every classroom [of Church of God schools] (42nd A., 1948, pp. 31, 32).

Commitment to Our Pentecostal Heritage

Our Pentecostal heritage and beliefs are increasingly scrutinized and discounted by those who seek to redefine our church in a manner which would give us an identity other than being a true Pentecostal church as found in the New Testament.

Therefore, we, the Church of God, go on record as making a renewal commitment to our Pentecostal heritage and beliefs, and to our Pentecostal statement of faith, in our Declaration of Faith, items 8 and 9:

8. In the baptism with the Holy Ghost subsequent to a clean heart.
9. In speaking with other tongues as the Spirit gives utterance and that it is the initial evidence of the baptism in the Holy Ghost (72nd A., 2008).

CHURCH OF GOD TEACHINGS

The Church of God stands for the whole Bible rightly divided. The New Testament is the only rule for government and discipline.

1. The Church of God stands now, as it has always stood, for the whole Bible rightly divided, and for the New Testament as the only rule for government and discipline. It has been necessary at times for the International General Assembly of the church to search the Scriptures and interpret the meaning of the Bible to arrive at what is the true and proper teaching of the church on various subjects, but always with the purpose and intention to base our teachings strictly upon the Bible.

2. For this purpose, a committee was appointed to report at the 1910 Assembly giving a collection of some of the teachings made prominent by the church, together with the Scriptures upon which these teachings were based; and that committee did report, and the matter contained in the report is set forth on page 47 of the printed *Minutes* of that Assembly.

3. However, the *Minutes* do not show that the report was officially adopted by the Assembly. The matters set forth in that report are simply a collection of some of the more important things that we have always believed, practiced, and taught, and is the law as set forth in the Holy Bible. We do not now attempt, and never have attempted, to make a law, but we have merely interpreted the Scriptures, and we have here set forth the laws that we have found there.

4. In order that there may be a record of the divine law, as set forth in the Scriptures, and as found and interpreted by the Assembly, it is now declared and reaffirmed that we accept and stand for the whole Bible rightly divided, and for the New Testament as our rule of faith and practice, and we do now declare the laws and teachings of the Bible, as set forth in the report of the said committee on page 47 of the 1910 *Minutes* of the General Assembly under the heading "Church of God Teachings" to be the official findings and interpretations of the 1930 Assembly of the Church of God upon the teachings and subjects thereon dealt with (25th A., 1930, p. 23).

5. *The Church of God Book of Discipline, Church Order, and Governance* shall be taught in all Church of God Bible schools and colleges, and ministerial students shall be required to take an examination equal to the questionnaire used in examining applicants for the ministry (43rd A., 1950, p. 18).

DOCTRINAL COMMITMENTS (55th A., 1974, p. 51; 67th A., 1998, p. 51)

1. Repentance. Mark 1:15; Luke 13:3; Acts 3:19 (DF 4).
2. Justification. Romans 5:1; Titus 3:7 (DF 5).
3. Regeneration. Titus 3:5 (DF 5).
4. New Birth. John 3:3; 1 Peter 1:23; 1 John 3:9 (DF 5).
5. Sanctification subsequent to Justification. Romans 5:2; 1 Corinthians 1:30; 1 Thessalonians 4:3; Hebrews 13:12 (DF 6).
6. Holiness. Luke 1:75; 1 Thessalonians 4:7; Hebrews 12:14 (DF 7).
7. Water baptism. Matthew 28:19; Mark 1:9, 10; John 3:22, 23; Acts 8:36, 38 (DF 10).
8. Baptism with the Holy Ghost subsequent to cleansing; the enduement of power for service. Matthew 3:11; Luke 24:49, 53; Acts 1:4-8 (DF 8).

9. The speaking in tongues as the Spirit gives utterance as the initial evidence of the baptism in the Holy Ghost. John 15:26; Acts 2:4; 10:44-46; 19:1-7 (DF 9).
10. The Church. Exodus 19:5, 6; Psalm 22:22; Matthew 16:13-19; 28:19, 20; Acts 1:8; 2:42-47; 7:38; 20:28; Romans 8:14-17; 1 Corinthians 3:16, 17; 12:12-31; 2 Corinthians 6:16-18; Ephesians 2:19-22; 3:9, 21; Philippians 3:10; Hebrews 2:12; 1 Peter 2:9; 1 John 1:6, 7; Revelation 21:2, 9; 22:17.
11. Spiritual gifts. 1 Corinthians 12:1, 7, 10, 28, 31; 14:1.
12. Signs following believers. Mark 16:17-20; Romans 15:18, 19; Hebrews 2:4.
13. Fruit of the Spirit. Romans 6:22; Galatians 5:22, 23; Ephesians 5:9; Philippians 1:11.
14. Divine healing provided for all in the Atonement. Psalm 103:3; Isaiah 53:4, 5; Matthew 8:17; James 5:14-16; 1 Peter 2:24 (DF 11).
15. The Lord's Supper. Luke 22:17-20; 1 Corinthians 11:23-26 (DF 12).
16. Washing the saints' feet. John 13:4-17; 1 Timothy 5:9, 10 (DF 12).
17. Tithing and giving. Genesis 14:18-20; 28:20-22; Malachi 3:10; Luke 11:42; 1 Corinthians 9:6-9; 16:2; Hebrews 7:1-21.
18. Restitution where possible. Matthew 3:8; Luke 19:8, 9.
19. Premillennial second coming of Jesus. First, to resurrect the dead saints and to catch away the living saints to Him in the air. 1 Corinthians 15:52; 1 Thessalonians 4:15-17; 2 Thessalonians 2:1. Second, To reign on the earth a thousand years. Zechariah 14:4; 1 Thessalonians 4:14; 2 Thessalonians 1:7-10; Jude 14, 15; Revelation 5:10; 19:11-21; 20:4-6 (DF 13, 14).
20. Resurrection. John 5:28, 29; Acts 24:15; Revelation 20:5, 6 (DF 3, 13, 14).
21. Eternal life for the righteous. Matthew 25:46; Luke 18:30; John 10:28; Romans 6:22; 1 John 5:11-13 (DF 14).
22. Eternal punishment for the wicked. No liberation nor annihilation. Matthew 25:41-46; Mark 3:29; 2 Thessalonians 1:8, 9; Revelation 20:10-15; 21:8 (DF 14).

RESOLUTION REGARDING DOCTRINAL AFFIRMATION

WHEREAS, the Church of God globally stands for the whole Bible rightly divided, and for the New Testament as the only rule of faith and practice; and

WHEREAS, the Church of God Declaration of Faith and Doctrinal Commitments remain the definitive statements of our beliefs; and

WHEREAS, we are living in a world that is constantly changing, and the calls to adapt our beliefs to prevailing societal norms or personal experiences are becoming more frequent;

BE IT THEREFORE RESOLVED, that we reaffirm our commitment to our core beliefs and values as stated in the latest edition of the book of *Minutes* of the Church of God International General Assembly—the *Church of God Book of Discipline, Church Order, and Governance;* and

BE IT FURTHER RESOLVED, that we communicate and emphasize the doctrinal distinctives of sanctification subsequent to the new birth, and baptism in the Holy Ghost subsequent to a clean heart; and

BE IT FURTHER RESOLVED, that we intentionally teach and proclaim our belief in the Pentecostal distinctive of speaking in other tongues as the initial evidence of the baptism in the Holy Spirit, and living a Spirit-empowered life; and

BE IT FURTHER RESOLVED, that our ministers prayerfully reaffirm their commitment to and belief in these doctrinal statements; and

BE IT FURTHER RESOLVED, that we continually seek to address current social issues in love, considering Biblical standards, not prevailing societal views; and

BE IT FURTHER RESOLVED, that to ensure generational continuity of faith, we instruct our youth in these doctrinal beliefs; and

BE IT FINALLY RESOLVED, that this resolution be placed in the book of *Minutes* following the **DOCTRINAL COMMITMENTS** (77th A., 2018).

PRACTICAL COMMITMENTS
(55th A., 1974, p. 51; 56th A., 1976, pp. 55, 56; 62nd A., 1988, Journal, p. 52)

I. SPIRITUAL EXAMPLE
We will demonstrate our commitment to Christ through our practice of the spiritual disciplines; we will demonstrate our commitment to the body of Christ through our loyalty to God and commitment to His church; and we will demonstrate our commitment to the work of Christ through our being good stewards.

A. Practice of Spiritual Disciplines

Spiritual disciplines involve such practices as prayer, praise, worship, confession, fasting, meditation, and study. Through prayer we express our trust in Jehovah God, the giver of all good things, and acknowledge our dependence on Him for our needs and for the needs of others (Matthew 6:5-15; Luke 11:1-13; James 5:13-18). Through both private and public worship we bless God, have communion with Him, and are provided daily with spiritual enrichment and growth in grace. Through periods of fasting we draw close to God, meditate on the passion of Christ, and discipline ourselves to submit to the control of the Holy Spirit in all areas of our life (Matthew 6:16-18; 9:14-17; Acts 14:23). Through confession of our sins to God we are assured of divine forgiveness (1 John 1:9—2:2). The sharing of our confession with other believers provides the opportunity to request prayer and to bear one another's burdens (Galatians 6:2; James 5:16). Through meditation on and study of the Word of God we enhance our own spiritual growth and prepare ourselves to help guide and instruct others in Scriptural truths (Joshua 1:8; Psalm 1:2; 2 Timothy 2:15, 23-26).

B. Loyalty to God and Commitment to the Church

The life of Christian discipleship calls for the fulfillment of our duties to the body of Christ. We are to unite regularly with other members of the church for the purpose of magnifying and praising God and hearing His Word (Matthew 18:20; John 4:23; Acts 2:42, 46, 47; 12:24; Hebrews 10:25). Sunday is the Christian day of worship. As the Lord's Day, it commemorates the resurrection of Christ from the dead (Matthew 28:1) and should be employed for worship, fellowship, Christian service, teaching, evangelism, and proclamation (Acts 20:7; Romans 14:5, 6; 1 Corinthians 16:2; Colossians 2:16, 17). We are to provide for the financial needs of the church by the giving of tithes (Malachi 3:10; Matthew 23:23) and offerings (1 Corinthians 16:2; 2 Corinthians 8:1-24; 9:1-15). It is our duty to respect and submit to those whom the Lord Jesus has placed over us in the church (1 Thessalonians 5:12, 13; Hebrews 13:7, 17). Our exercise of authority must be as a spiritual example rather than as a lord over God's flock (Matthew 20:25-28; 1 Peter 5:1-3). Furthermore, our submission must be a manifestation of the spiritual grace of humility (Ephesians 5:21; 1 Peter 5:5, 6). Finally, we are to avoid affiliation with oath-bound societies. Such societies may appear to have spiritual character, but by being oath-bound and secretive, they contradict Christian spirituality (John 18:20; 2 Corinthians 6:14-18). Christians must not belong to any body or society that requires or practices an allegiance that supersedes or excludes their fellowship in Christ (Matthew 12:47-49; John 17:21-23).

C. Being Good Stewards

In the Scriptures, the virtues of thrift and simplicity are honored, but the vices of waste and ostentation are solemnly prohibited (Isaiah 55:2; Matthew 6:19-23). The living of a godly and sober life requires the wise and frugal use of our temporal blessings, including time, talent, and money. As good stewards we are to make the most of our time, whether for recreation or for work (Ephesians 5:16; Colossians 4:5). The idle use of leisure time degrades (2 Thessalonians 3:6-13; 1 Timothy 5:13), but the edifying use of it brings inner renewal. All our work and play should honor the name of God (1 Corinthians 10:31). As good stewards we must use fully our spiritual gifts (Romans 12:3-8; 1 Corinthians 12:1-11, 27-31; Ephesians 4:11-16; 1 Peter 4:9-11) and natural talents (Matthew 25:14-30) for the glory of God. As good stewards we must recognize that the wise use of money is an essential part of the Christian's economy of life. God has committed temporal blessings to our trust (Matthew 7:11; James 1:17).

II. MORAL PURITY

We will engage in those activities which glorify God in our body and which avoid the fulfillment of the lust of the flesh. We will read, watch, and listen to those things which are of positive benefit to our spiritual well-being.

A. Glorifying God in Our Body

Our body is the temple of the Holy Ghost, and we are to glorify God in our body (Romans 12:1, 2; 1 Corinthians 6:19, 20; 10:31). We are to walk in the Spirit and not fulfill the lust of the flesh (Galatians 5:16). Examples of fleshly behavior which do not glorify God are noted in several passages of Scripture (Romans 1:24; 1 Corinthians 6:9, 10; Galatians 5:19-21; Revelation 21:8). Sinful practices which are made prominent and condemned in these scriptures include homosexuality, adultery, worldly attitudes (such as hatred, envy, jealousy), corrupt communication (such as gossip, angry outbursts, filthy words), stealing, murder, drunkenness, and witchcraft. Witchcraft has to do with the practices of the occult, which are forbidden by God and lead to the worship of Satan.

B. Reading, Watching, and Listening

The literature we read, the programs we watch, and the music we listen to profoundly affect the way we feel, think, and behave. It is imperative, then, that the Christian read, watch, and listen to those things which inspire, instruct, and challenge to a higher plane of living. Therefore, literature, programs, and music which are worldly in content or pornographic in nature must be avoided. A Christian is not to attend (or watch on television) movies or theatrical performances of a demoralizing nature (Romans 13:14; Philippians 4:8).

C. Benefiting Spiritual Well-being

The use of leisure time in the life of a Christian should be characterized by those activities which edify both the individual and the body of Christ (Romans 6:13; 1 Corinthians 10:31, 32). We are to avoid places and practices which are of this world. Consequently, a Christian must not be a part of any other types of entertainment which appeal to the fleshly nature and/or bring discredit to the Christian testimony (2 Corinthians 6:17; 1 Thessalonians 5:21, 22; 1 John 2:15-17).

III. PERSONAL INTEGRITY

We will live in a manner that inspires trust and confidence, bearing the fruit of the Spirit, and seeking to manifest the character of Christ in all our behavior.

A. Trust and Confidence

A Christian should be trustworthy, dependable, and a person of his word (Matthew 5:37; 1 Peter 2:11, 12). Therefore, the swearing of oaths is contrary to a Christian's trustworthiness and should be avoided (Matthew 5:34-37; James 5:12). Christ, by precept and example, taught that we love our enemy and prefer our brother

(Matthew 5:43-48; Romans 12:10; Philippians 2:3; 1 John 3:16). We should behave in a way that will point others to Christ (Matthew 5:16; 1 Corinthians 11:1).

B. Fruit of the Spirit

If we live in the Spirit, we will manifest the fruit (attitudes and actions) of the Spirit and will not fulfill the lusts of the flesh (Galatians 5:16, 22-25; 1 John 1:7). Trustful relationships with others are a natural outgrowth of our positive relationship with the Lord (Psalm 1:1-3; Matthew 22:37-40). A lack of fruit-bearing in our lives will be judged (Matthew 7:16-20; Luke 13:6-9; John 15:1-8).

C. Character of Christ

Love for others is the hallmark of the Christ-life (John 13:34, 35; 15:9-13; 1 John 4:7-11). In His relationship with His Father, Jesus displayed submission (Luke 22:42; John 4:34; 5:30). In His relationship with others, He demonstrated acceptance (John 8:11), compassion (Matthew 9:36; Mark 6:34), and forgiveness (Matthew 9:2; Luke 5:20). We cannot bear the fruit of the Spirit and manifest the character of Christ without being spiritually joined to Christ (John 15:4, 5) and without having the seed of the Word planted in our heart (John 15:3; 1 Peter 1:22, 23).

IV. FAMILY RESPONSIBILITY

We will give priority to fulfilling family responsibilities, to preserving the sanctity of marriage, and to maintaining divine order in the home.

A. Priority of the Family

The family is the basic unit of human relationship and as such is foundational to both society and the church (Genesis 2:18-24). The divine origin of the family, along with its foundational character, makes it imperative that we give priority to ministry to the family, both from a personal and corporate standpoint. The practice of Christian disciplines and virtues should begin in the home (Deuteronomy 6:6, 7). Therefore, our families should establish some pattern for family devotions and should endeavor to provide a Christian environment in the home (1 Timothy 3:3, 4; 5:8).

B. Sanctity of Marriage

Marriage is ordained of God and is a spiritual union in which a man and a woman are joined by God to live together as one (Genesis 2:24; Mark 10:7). Because of the divine character of marriage, it is a lifelong commitment with the only clear Biblical allowance for divorce being fornication (Matthew 5:32; 19:9).

Sexual involvement either before marriage or with someone other than the marriage partner is strictly forbidden in Scripture (Exodus 20:14; 1 Corinthians 6:15-18). Understanding the sanctity of marriage, partners should strive to maintain a happy, harmonious, and holy relationship. Should divorce occur, the church should be quick to provide love, understanding, and counsel to those involved. The remarriage of divorced persons should be undertaken only after a thorough understanding of and submission to the Scriptural instructions concerning this issue (Matthew 19:7-9; Mark 10:2-12; Luke 16:18; Romans 7:2, 3; 1 Corinthians 7:2, 10, 11). Should a Christian desire to remain single, this decision should be respected and should be seen as a viable Scriptural alternative (1 Corinthians 7:8, 32-34).

C. Divine Order in the Home

When God created man, He created them male and female (Genesis 1:27). He gave them distinctly different characteristics (1 Corinthians 11:14, 15; 1 Peter 3:7) as well as different responsibilities (Genesis 3:16-19; 1 Peter 3:1-7). In God's order the husband is head of the home (Ephesians 5:22-31; Colossians 3:18, 19), parents are to nurture and admonish their children (Ephesians 6:4, Colossians 3:21), and children are to obey and honor their parents (Exodus 20:12; Ephesians 6:1-3; Colossians 3:20). In order for harmony to exist in the home, God's order of responsibility must be observed.

V. Behavioral Temperance

We will practice temperance in behavior and will abstain from activities and attitudes which are offensive to our fellowman or which lead to addiction or enslavement.

A. Temperance

One of the cardinal Christian virtues is temperance or self-control (1 Corinthians 9:25; Titus 1:8; 2:2). It is listed as fruit of the Spirit (Galatians 5:23). We are admonished to practice moderation and balance in our behavior (Philippians 4:5). The Scripture indicates that it is within our prerogative to control our thinking (Philippians 4:8), our anger (Ephesians 4:26), and our communication (Ephesians 4:29; Colossians 3:8). To exercise self-discipline reflects the power of God in our life (1 Corinthians 9:27; 2 Peter 1:5-11).

B. Offensive Behavior

The Bible speaks clearly that we are to be sensitive to the needs and feelings of others as a demonstration of our love for them

(Matthew 22:39; Romans 12:9-21; 13:10; Philippians 2:3-5). At times it is necessary for us to control our behavior so as not to bring offense to others (Romans 14:13-21; 1 Corinthians 8:9-13). As we know Christ after the Spirit, we are also to know others in the same manner so we will not judge them after their outward behavior alone (2 Corinthians 5:16). A respect and tolerance for differences in others should characterize our relationships (Romans 14:2, 3; 1 Corinthians 8:8; Ephesians 4:2; Colossians 3:13; 1 Timothy 4:1-5).

C. Addiction and Enslavement

One of the primary benefits of our liberty in Christ is freedom from the domination of negative forces (John 8:32, 36; Romans 6:14; 8:2). We are counseled not to put ourselves again under bondage (Galatians 5:1). Therefore, a Christian must totally abstain from all alcoholic beverages and other habit-forming and mood-altering chemical substances and refrain from the use of tobacco in any form, marijuana, and all other addictive substances and, further, must refrain from any activity (such as gambling or gluttony) which defiles the body as the temple of God or which dominates and enslaves the spirit that has been made free in Christ (Proverbs 20:1; 23:20-35; Isaiah 28:7; 1 Corinthians 3:17; 5:11; 6:10; 2 Corinthians 7:1; James 1:21).

VI. MODEST APPEARANCE

We will demonstrate the Scriptural principle of modesty by appearing and dressing in a manner that will enhance our Christian testimony and will avoid pride, elaborateness, or sensuality.

A. Modesty

According to the Biblical idea, modesty is an inner spiritual grace that recoils from anything unseemly and impure, is chaste in thought and conduct, and is free of crudeness and indecency in dress and behavior (Ephesians 4:25, 29, 31; 5:1-8; 1 Timothy 2:9, 10). Therefore, modesty includes our appearance, dress, speech, and conduct and can be applied to all situations. The essential issue is, does our style of life please or displease God?

B. Appearance and Dress

Our life, character, and self-image are reflected by our apparel and mode of dress. The admonition of Scripture, "Be not conformed to this world," reminds us that our manner of dress must be modest and decent (Romans 12:2; 1 Thessalonians 5:22, 23). It is not displeasing to God for us to dress well and be well groomed. However, above all we must seek spiritual beauty, which does not come from outward adornment with jewelry, expensive clothes, or cosmetics, but from good works, chaste conversation, and a meek and quiet spirit (Philippians 4:8; 1 Peter 3:3-5).

C. Pride, Elaborateness, Sensuality

As godly people we are to abstain from all lusts of the flesh and avoid dressing in a manner that encourages immoral thoughts, attitudes, and lifestyles (Galatians 5:13-21; 1 Peter 2:11; 2 Peter 1:4). Our beauty does not depend on elaborate, showy dress; extravagant, costly attire; or on the use of jewelry or cosmetics but on our relationship with Christ. External adornment, whether clothing or jewelry, as an outward display of personal worth, is contrary to a spiritual attitude (James 2:1-4).

VII. SOCIAL OBLIGATION

It should be our objective to fulfill our obligations to society by being good citizens, by correcting social injustices, and by protecting the sanctity of life.

A. Being Good Citizens

As Christians we are members of the kingdom of God as well as a social order of this world. Obedience to God requires us to act in a responsible manner as citizens of our country (Mark 12:13-17; Romans 13:1-7; 1 Peter 2:13-17). Therefore, we should support civil law and order; hold our leaders in respect and pray for them; participate in school, community, and governmental activities; exercise our voting rights; and speak out on clear-cut moral issues. God's law is supreme, but we are to obey the laws of our country insofar as they are not in conflict with obedience to God (Acts 5:29). When it becomes necessary to disagree with practices and requirements of government, we should do so out of a concern for the promotion of righteousness and not out of delight in discord and controversy.

B. Correcting Social Injustices

Love for others and the recognition of the equal worth of all people in the sight of God (Acts 10:34; 17:26) should compel us to take steps to improve the situation of those who are underprivileged, neglected, hungry, homeless, and victimized by prejudice, persecution, and oppression (Matthew 22:39; Romans 13:8-10; 1 John

3:17). In all of our dealings, we must be sensitive to human needs (Luke 10:30-37; James 1:17) and guard against racial and economic discrimination. Every person should have freedom to worship and participate in the life of the church regardless of race, color, sex, social class, or nationality.

C. Protecting the Sanctity of Life

God alone confers life (Genesis 1:1-31); therefore, we are responsible to God to care for our physical life and that of others. If the circumstances require, we must be prepared to risk our life in the service of our neighbor (John 15:13); but the general rule is that we must respect our physical life and employ every worthy means to maintain it. Since God alone confers life, God alone must decide when it is to be ended (Psalm 31:14, 15). Because a human fetus is sacred and blessed of God, we believe we have the responsibility to protect the life of the unborn (Jeremiah 1:5; Luke 1:41). It is our firm conviction that abortion, and euthanasia of the aged, mentally incompetent, terminally ill, and otherwise handicapped, for reasons of personal convenience, social adjustment, or economic advantage, are morally wrong. Furthermore, we believe it is our Christian responsibility to care for the earth and its resources. In the beginning God gave man dominion over the earth (Genesis 1:26-30). This does not, however, give us license to pollute our natural environment or to waste the resources of the earth.

EXPLANATORY NOTES

I. NEW BIRTH

1. "Except a man be born of water and of the Spirit, he cannot enter into the kingdom of God" (John 3:5).

2. Is being born of water a natural or a spiritual birth? Natural, "that which is born of the flesh is flesh; and that which is born of the Spirit is spirit" (John 3:6) (20th A., 1925, p. 39; DF 5, 6; CT 4).

II. ORDINANCES OF THE CHURCH

A. Water Baptism

1. Water baptism is to plunge or dip, or a burial beneath the surface of the water and a lifting out again (6th A., 1911, p. 6).

2. Water baptism is not a door into the church, but an act of obedience after one has been converted (7th A., 1912, p. 19).

3. We recognize immersion as the Scriptural mode of water baptism. We recommend that our disciples be baptized by a minister who is baptized in the Holy Ghost. However, inasmuch as the apostles baptized before and after Pentecost, we leave this matter with the conscience of the individual, and we should not exclude them if they are satisfied with their baptism, provided they have been baptized in the name of the Father, and of the Son, and of the Holy Ghost (10th A., 1914, p. 26; 28th A., 1933, p. 43).

4. That water baptism be administered by ordained ministers or bishops, and that it be in accordance with the commission given by Jesus in Matthew 28:19: "Baptizing them in the name of the Father, and of the Son, and of the Holy Ghost" (39th A., 1944, p. 30; DF 10; CT 7).

5. That we authorize the printing of certificates of baptism and recommend that they be issued to those baptized by the officiating minister (41st A., 1946, p. 26).

B. Lord's Supper (Communion) and Feet Washing

The subject of Communion and Feet Washing was considered and the Assembly decided that both are taught in the New Testament and may be engaged in at the same service or at different times at the option of the local churches. In order to preserve the unity of the body, and to obey the sacred Word, it was recommended that every member engage in these sacred services, which should be observed one or more times each year (1st A., 1906, Bk. M., p. 15; DF 12).

III. Family Worship

Family worship was considered and the Assembly recommended and urged that the families of all the churches engage in this very sacred and important service at least once a day, and at a time most convenient to the household, and that the parents should see that every child is taught as early as possible to reverence God and his parents, by listening quietly and attentively to the reading of God's Word and getting down on his knees during the prayer. The pastor and deacons of each church were advised to use their influence and make special efforts to encourage every family in the church to engage in this devotional exercise every day (1st A., 1906, Bk. M., p. 17).

IV. Divorce and Remarriage

1. That all former rulings on divorce and remarriage be revised to read as follows: All parties who have put their companions away for the cause of fornication, having been divorced and remarried,

provided they are otherwise qualified, are eligible for membership in the Church of God (28th A., 1933, pp. 43, 44; Amended 33rd A., 1938, p. 50).

2. Inasmuch as the divorce evil has grown to such alarming proportions and since the Church of God is a holiness institution divinely ordained to serve the best interests of the human race, therefore, be it resolved that we reaffirm our traditional position regarding the sanctity of the home and the sacredness of marriage vows, both of which should be held inviolate for the protection of our national security. Inasmuch as we also consider such present social trends to be detrimental to the home, the church, and the nation, be it further resolved that the minister be an example of Christian chastity and that his marital status be above question. The Church of God must have the highest type ministry—a ministry whose moral and spiritual experiences provide the incentive to develop the Christian character indispensable to the national honor of our republic and the preservation of our Christian principles (43rd A., 1950, p. 18).

V. Lodges and Fraternal Orders

1. The Church of God teaches against members belonging to lodges.

2. Should anyone unite with the church who has insurance with a fraternal or secret order, he may continue his insurance with said order, provided he does not attend their secret meetings (35th A., 1940, pp. 31, 32).

VI. Divine Healing

We recommend that our people in testifying to divine healing refrain from using expressions making thrusts at physicians or the use of medicine. Preach and testify to divine healing as a privilege, giving God the glory (24th A., 1929, p. 35).

VII. Combatant Military Service

The Church of God believes that nations can and should settle their differences without going to war; however, in the event of war, if a member engages in combatant service, it will not affect his status with the church. In case a member is called into military service who has conscientious objections to combatant service, the church will support him in his constitutional rights (23rd A., 1928, p. 24 (2); 40th A., 1945, p. 31).

VIII. Tobacco

This Assembly agreed to stand with one accord in opposition to the use of tobacco in any form (1st A., 1906, Bk. M., p. 16; 56th A., 1976, p. 48).

IX. QUESTION AND ANSWER
Q. Should those who do not pay tithes have a voice in the church?
A. If a member does not have enough interest in the church to support it with his tithes, he should have respect enough for the church to keep quiet in business meetings (22nd A., 1927, p. 32).

RESOLUTION RELATIVE TO PRINCIPLES OF HOLINESS OF CHURCH OF GOD
(48th A., 1960, pp. 51, 52; 56th A., 1976; DF 7; CT 6; 65th A., 1994, pp. 124, 125)

The foundation of the Church of God is laid upon the principles of Biblical holiness. Even before the church experienced the outpouring of the Holy Ghost, its roots were set in the holiness revival of the past century. It was, and is, a holiness church—holiness in fact and holiness in name.

The passing of 90 years has not diminished our holiness position or convictions. The years have, instead, strengthened our knowledge that without holiness it is impossible to please God.

We hereby remind ourselves that the Scriptures enjoin us at all times to examine our own hearts. The continuing and consistent life of holiness requires this. Conditions of our day desperately require it. The subtle encroachment of worldliness is a very real and unrelenting threat to the church. We must therefore beware lest we become conformed to the world, or lest a love for the world take root in our hearts to manifest itself as lust of the flesh, lust of the eye, or the pride of life.

For these reasons, we present the following:

WHEREAS, the Church of God is historically a holiness church; and

WHEREAS, we are enjoined by the Scriptures to be so; and

WHEREAS, a tide of worldliness threatens the spirituality of the church;

BE IT RESOLVED that we, the Church of God, reaffirm our standard of holiness, in stated doctrine, in principles of conduct, and as a living reality in our hearts; and

BE IT FURTHER RESOLVED that we, the Church of God, believe a life of holiness is a balanced life in spirit, mind, and body, and that it places the believer in a Christlike relationship to God and fellowmen; and

BE IT FURTHER RESOLVED that we, as ministers, maintain this standard in our own lives, in our homes, and in our pulpits; and

BE IT FURTHER RESOLVED that we, as ministers and members, rededicate ourselves to this purpose, and guard our lives against conformity to the world in appearance, in selfish ambition, in carnal attitudes, and in evil associations; and

BE IT FURTHER RESOLVED that we, as ministers and members, seek to conform to the positive virtues of love, mercy, and forgiveness as taught by Jesus Christ.

SCRIPTURAL PRINCIPLES FOR MINISTRY

(65th A., 1994, Item 2, pp. 78-83; 71st A., 2006, p. 44)

PREAMBLE

Begun in 1886, the Church of God has been signally blessed of God. The growth of the church is attributable to a number of factors. Some of the most significant are (1) obedience to the Word of God; (2) reliance upon the Holy Spirit; (3) faithfulness to our call; (4) evangelistic fervor; (5) openness to all people; (6) missionary outreach; (7) discipleship training; and (8) a deep desire to retain the roots of Pentecostal worship, prayer, revival, and holiness.

As with other religious organizations, we now face great and complex challenges. About us are undeniable signs that tough times lie ahead for any movement attempting to survive and grow with an attitude of business as usual. We must take an honest look at our challenges, and we must not complacently assume immunity to the difficulties faced by other larger, more traditional denominations, some of which are already in the embrace of noticeable decline.

We fully accept the uniqueness of our position as one of the leading Pentecostal churches in the world. We see ourselves as a divine work of the Holy Spirit, a vital part of a spiritual movement called to help usher in revival and bring renewal to a spiritually hungry world.

For all of us, this is an awesome and sobering responsibility.

STATEMENT OF VISION

Our vision arises from our understanding of what the sovereign God purposes to do for and through His church. The Great Commission remains our mandate from Christ.

The Church of God is to be:

1. A movement committed to the authority of Holy Scripture for faith and direction.
2. A fellowship whose worship brings God's power into the life of the church and extends that power through the lives of believers into the marketplace of life.
3. A body that is directed by the Spirit, fully understanding that baptism in the Holy Spirit is both a personal blessing and an endowment of power for witness and service in fulfilling the Great Commission.
4. A people who hunger for God, experience the presence of God, and stand in awe of His holiness as He changes believers into conformity with Christ.
5. A New Testament church which focuses on the local congregation where the pastor nurtures and leads all members to exercise spiritual gifts in ministry.
6. A church that loves all people and stands opposed to any action or policy that discriminates against any group or individual because of race, color, or nationality.
7. A movement that evidences love and concern for the hurts and loneliness of the unsaved through aggressive evangelistic, discipling, and nurturing ministries.
8. A church that is Christ-centered, people-oriented, and need-sensitive in all its programs and ministries.
9. A movement that promotes policies and ministries which reflect an open, sincere effort to remain relevant to each generation.

STATEMENT OF MISSION

The mission of the Church of God is to communicate the full gospel of Jesus Christ (Matthew 28:19, 20) in the Spirit and power of Pentecost (Acts 2:1-4, 6, 13-18) (71st A., 2006, p. 44).

COMMITMENTS TO OUR MISSION AND VISION

(70th A., 2004, pp. 50-54; 75th A., 2014, pp. 184-86)

These items reflect our core values in regard to fulfilling our mission and vision.

1. PRAYER

We commit ourselves to making prayer the highest priority of the church demonstrated by:

Every local church becoming a house of prayer for all nations.

Emphasizing communication with God as the highest privilege and greatest responsibility of every member.

Modeling by all church leadership of an active and effective prayer life.

Uniting with other believers in corporate and intercessory prayer.

(Isaiah. 56:7; Mark 11:17; Romans. 8:26; 1 Corinthians 14:14, 15; 1 Thessalonians 5:17; 1 Timothy 2:1-4, 8; James 5:14, 15)

2. PENTECOSTAL WORSHIP

We commit ourselves to gather regularly as the local expression of the Body of Christ to participate in Pentecostal worship that exalts God, engages the heart, mind, and soul, and challenges to deeper commitment and discipleship. This commitment will be demonstrated by:

Assisting local churches in planning and preparing for meaningful, anointed worship.

Equipping pastors and other worship leaders to lead authentically expressed, spiritually alive worship.

Modeling varying styles and forms of worship that glorify God and encouraging outreach and service.

Emphasizing the importance of Biblical stewardship and the centrality of God's Word as elements of worship.

(John 4:24; Psalm 29:2; Romans 12:1; 1 Corinthians 12:4-11; Isaiah 58; Matthew 25:31-46)

3. WORLD EVANGELIZATION

We commit ourselves to intentionally reaching the unconverted, baptizing them in water, and leading them to unite with the church. This commitment will be demonstrated by:

Viewing all the nations of the world as our mission field.

Encouraging our local churches to adopt and intercede for an unreached people group. Resource materials will be provided by the Ministry of World Missions.

Asking all national churches of the Church of God international to adopt and implement measurable steps to evangelize and disciple unreached people groups inside and outside of their own regions (Matthew 28:18-20; Romans 15:19-24; Revelation 5:9).

Encouraging every local church to increase a minimum of 10 percent per year through conversion growth.

Cultivating a genuine passion for the lost that will compel members to personally communicate the gospel of Jesus and demonstrate His love to those outside the faith.

Discipling new believers and passing on our faith to the next generation.

Practicing lifestyle evangelism.

(Matthew 9:37-38; Matthew 28:19-20; Mark 16:15-18; Acts 1:8; Romans 10:13-15)

4. CHURCH PLANTING

We commit ourselves to identifying, training, and resourcing God-called church planters and to intentionally planting new life-giving churches. This commitment will be demonstrated by:

Focusing designated resources of the local church, state/regional offices, and the International Offices for planting new churches

Starting the number of church plants equal to a minimum of 3 percent of the total number of churches in a state/region/nation annually.

Developing a certified training program in our Ministry of USA Missions and educational institutions for church planters and home missions.

Emphasizing the health and viability of new church plants as well as the number of churches planted.

Affirming the different models of church planting for different situations.

Recognizing church planting as an apostolic ministry for our day.
(Matthew 16:18; John 4:35; Acts 2:47; 14:23; Ephesians 5:25-28)

5. LEADERSHIP DEVELOPMENT

We commit ourselves to identifying and developing individuals whom God has called and given leadership gifts and challenging them to become servant-leaders. We will demonstrate our commitment by:

Creating an environment in which men and women with ministry gifts are developed to serve as servant-leaders.

Equipping, empowering, and releasing lay leaders to serve as ministry partners both inside and outside the local church.

Providing relevant resources and training opportunities for both clergy and laity.

Encouraging pastors to lead through vision, to communicate the vision to the congregation, and to organize the body and each of its ministry groups so the vision can be realized. (Mark 3:13-15; 2 Timothy 2:2; 2:15; 3:14-17; Ephesians 4:11-13)

6. CARE

We commit ourselves to the challenge of being a church that genuinely cares for one another and for those who are lost, hurting, and needy. We will demonstrate our commitment by:

Building loving, caring relationships within families, between members, and within the communities we serve.

Obeying the Care Commission of Christ in Matthew 25.

Cultivating compassion and showing mercy to the unloved, the undesirable, and the unreached of our society.

Establishing in each local church some type of outreach ministry that demonstrates our genuine concern and love for the disadvantaged or oppressed. (Psalms 86:15; Matthew 25; Luke 6:36; Acts 20:28)

7. INTERDEPENDENCE

We commit ourselves to the principle of interdependence, acknowledging our interconnectedness and dependence on all the members of the Body of Christ. We will demonstrate our commitment by:

Reaching out to others in the Body of Christ for collaboration, resource sharing, and learning opportunities.

Encouraging local churches to build relationships with like-minded and like-hearted churches in their communities to work together to reach the lost.

Involving clergy in the processes of mentoring, coaching, and consulting on the local, state, regional, national and international levels to increase the level of trust and support among ministers.

Engaging in dialogue and partnership with local, national, and international organizations who seek to fulfill the Great Commission of Christ. (Colossians 2:19; 1 Corinthians 12:14-31; Galatians 6:1-6)

8. COMMUNICATION

That we commit ourselves to utilizing every available medium and means to effectively maintain open and perpetual communication with our constituency. This commitment will be demonstrated by:

Understanding that communication is the process of exchanging information, imparting ideas, and sharing the message so it is understood by others.

Exploring the best media choices available to enable the transforming message of Christ to all mankind and cultural contexts.

Discovering new ways and means of efficient and effective electronic mediums to maintain continuous connection with our constituency.

Empowering ministry resources available to the church for immediate response to the needs of the world and the mission engagement of the church.

Employing every facet of communication to expand the global reach of Christ's message, sustaining open exchange of ministry concepts, encouraging the strengthening and growth of local churches, enlisting and equipping the next generation of leaders, and fulfilling our mission and vision as a movement that is Christ-centered, people-oriented, and need-sensitive in all its ministry endeavors (75th A., 2014).

9. DISCIPLESHIP

We commit ourselves to the Lord's command to make disciples of all nations, to develop committed and faithful followers of Jesus Christ, and to be people of conviction identifiable by:

1. Their commitment to know what they believe and who they are in Christ;

2. Their competence through spiritual discipline, calling, and empowerment, and;

3. Their character development, which will result in reproducing themselves, disciples making disciples.

This commitment will be demonstrated by:

Understanding that discipleship must be intentional for all believers upon their acceptance of Jesus Christ as personal Savior. If we are to retain them, they must be taught and have someone who will disciple them.

Asking every church to prioritize discipleship in every facet of their ministry. Everything that is planned and executed in the local church should be identified as part of the discipleship process for those who are involved. The local church must understand that the growth process is ever evolving and must provide a framework by which growth can happen.

Providing resources and discipleship experiences that will assist pastors and church leaders in the discipleship process, understanding that models may vary, but the outcome will be committed Christ followers.

Understanding that passing the faith to the next generation will require making disciples of all ages. Discipleship must begin at the earliest age and continue.
(Matthew 5:43-48; 22:37-38; 28:19-20; John 14:15, 21-23; 15:10; Acts 1:8; 2:1-11, 41-47; Romans 12:1-2; 12:3-8; 1 Corinthians 12:4-11; Galatians 5:22-25; 1 Thessalonians 5:19-23; 2 John 6) (75th A., 2014).

10. EDUCATION

We commit ourselves to education as a vital part of all phases of the Spirit-filled Christian life. Education is to be nurtured by the church: locally in rural areas, towns, and cities; regionally in counties, states, and geographical regions; internationally in every country with a Church of God presence; and globally on every continent of the world. We will demonstrate our commitment by:

Developing and fostering means of self-education with access to educational resources.

Recognizing local-church institutions which provide education in church and/or school formats.

Affirming in public places those who minister in education.

Sponsoring educational institutions of higher learning to equip laity, ministers, institutions, and ministries.

Providing curriculum and materials which affirm the doctrines, practices, mission, vision, and commitments of the Church of God (75th A., 2014).

LOCAL CHURCH

A. Priority Statement: The Church of God recognizes the local church as the foundation of all ministry activities and will renew efforts to acknowledge, affirm, strengthen, and support the central importance of the ministry of the local church.

B. For Implementation We Recommend:
1. More open proclamation of the joy and power of worship (Isaiah 6:1-4; Psalms 147:1; 149:1; 150:1-6; John 4:23, 24; 9:31; Revelation 11:16).
2. Prayerful search for clearer understanding of spiritual gifts and their operation in the church (1 Corinthians 12:1-11; 14:1-40; Romans 12:4-8).
3. Greater care in the appointment of pastors, with emphasis on compatibility and interrelationships between congregation and leaders (Titus 1:5-9; Ephesians 5:21; Hebrews 13:17, 18; Romans 12:14-21).
4. Strengthening the pastor in his role as spiritual shepherd with first responsibility for prayer and ministry of the Word (Acts 6:4; 2 Timothy 2:15).
5. More emphasis on teaching pastors to train and involve lay men and women for effective ministry (Ephesians 4:11-16; 1 Timothy 4:11-16; 5:17; 1 Peter 4:10, 11).
6. Development of a method for objective evaluation of local church ministries (2 Corinthians 13:1-3, 5; Colossians 1:9-20).

LAITY

A. Priority Statement: The Church of God will further emphasize the doctrinal position of the priesthood of all believers and will encourage laity to assume a rightful Biblical role as full partners in ministry throughout every area of the church.

B. For Implementation We Recommend:
1. Renewed and expanded efforts by all pastors to train, inspire, equip and release laypeople for ministry in strategic

areas of local church and community service (Acts 6:1-7; Ephesians 4:11-16; 1 Thessalonians 1:4-10).
2. Specific steps for defining and developing the ministry of deacons and elders (Acts 6:1-7; 1 Timothy 3:8-13; Titus 1:5-9).
3. Joint sessions between lay and ministerial leadership in establishing harvest goals and objectives for the Church of God.
4. Continued study as to the role of laity in the International General Assembly of the Church of God.

CLERGY

A. Priority Statement: The Church of God believes that from within the priesthood of all believers God specifically selects, calls, anoints, and commissions certain individuals for extraordinary service and leadership and that this special (clergy) calling is of God's sovereign will, characterized by individuals with spiritual passion, love for the lost, total involvement, lifelong sacrifice, and servant leadership rather than by those seeking position or personal honor.

B. For Implementation We Recommend:
1. More emphasis upon local church confirmation, affirmation, and endorsement of ministerial applicants prior to their seeking exhorter's license (Acts 13:1-4; 14:23).
2. Establishing more specific Scriptural and practical assessment and appraisal procedures for evaluating ministers of all ranks and in all positions on a continuing basis (Romans 12:2; 13:5; 2 Timothy 4:5).
3. Heightened emphasis on continuing education for all ministers through formal institutions and special seminars, study programs, and conventions (2 Timothy 2:15).
4. Recognition of the vital role women presently give in Church of God ministry—their teaching, preaching, administrative and leadership skills—and renewed encouragement and support for their ministry, in keeping with that obvious emphasis found in the Gospels, throughout the Book of Acts, and in the Epistles (Acts 16:14, 15, 40; 18:26; 21:8, 9; Romans 16:1-7; Titus 2:3-5).

LEADERSHIP

A. Priority Statement: The Church of God believes leaders must exemplify the servant qualities of Jesus (Matthew 20:27, 28; Philippians 2:17), that they must conform to the highest moral and ethical standards (Titus 1:5-9), and that they must place the welfare of others before that of themselves (John 10:11; 1 Peter 5:2).

B. For Implementation We Recommend:
1. That full honor, respect, and recognition be given to the Holy Spirit, who is Himself the true leader of the church (Acts 13:4; 15:28; 16:6, 7).
2. Greater attention to personal accountability and positional responsibility on the part of all leaders, with Scriptural emphasis on caring (pastoral) relationships (1 Corinthians 12:25; Colossians 4:17; 1 Timothy 3:15; Hebrews 13:17).
3. More emphasis on the Scriptural qualifications for bishop (1 Timothy 3:1-7; Titus 1:5-9) and greater care in the leadership selection and appointment process.
4. More delegating of secondary matters (Acts 6:3) in order to keep the role of bishop in perspective (Acts 6:4).
5. More focus by the leadership in the utilization of ministry resources and skills of retired clergy at the local, district, state, and national levels (Romans 13:7).

CONSECRATION

A. Priority Statement: The Church of God resolutely declares that its accomplishments can never be truly reflected in numerical growth, physical accomplishments, or the adulation of men; but our true success as God's church is always measured in terms of our relationship with God through Jesus Christ.

B. For Implementation We Recommend:
1. Renewal of our pledge to do whatever is necessary to be God's people on this earth (Ephesians 3:14-21).
2. Periodic calls throughout the church for solemn assemblies (Joel 2:15-17) which involve confession, repentance, dedication, and obedience to the voice of God (2 Chronicles 7:14; Romans 12:1; James 4:8-10).

3. Reaffirmation of our belief and daily practice of Biblical holiness and personal integrity (1 Corinthians 7:34; 2 Corinthians 7:1; Colossians 1:21, 22; 1 Thessalonians 2:7, 8; 2 Timothy 1:9; Hebrews 12:14).
4. That our clergy and laity seek for vision and passion, both of which are born in and maintained by prayer (Joel 2:28; Acts 26:19; Romans 9:2, 3; 1 Thessalonians 2:7, 8).
5. A renewed commitment to become more responsive to the voice of God to our society for justice, righteousness, and all other Scriptural principles rather than a mere echo of popular opinion (Luke 3:4; Acts 4:10-12; Ephesians 6:20; 1 Thessalonians 5:20; Micah 6:6-12; Amos 5:1-27).

COMMISSION ON ORGANIZATION REPORT
(65th A., 1994, Item 3, pp. 83-85)

LOCAL CHURCH
1. That we acknowledge the local church as God's primary force in the evangelization of the world and discipling of believers in the fulfillment of the Great Commission.
2. That each local church follow the Scriptural pattern in developing a ministry of elders and deacons, identifying, training, and setting forth those individuals gifted in these ministries.
3. That the general church constituency be given the opportunity to evaluate the present pastoral selection and appointment process.

DISTRICT
1. That we reaffirm the value, visibility, and authority of the district overseer. And, further, that the state overseer consult with the district overseer before the appointment of a pastor on his district.
2. That a district overseer's manual be developed and updated on a regular basis.
3. That the work of the district overseer be evaluated on an annual basis.

STATE/REGIONAL
1. That a policy relative to boundaries (geographical, ethnic, linguistic) which allows for smaller states or regions to be consolidated with one another or with adjoining supporting states or regions

to form a supporting entity be developed and implemented in order to promote growth in ministry.
2. That when state or regional properties such as campgrounds and/or recreational areas are to be purchased or sold, the ministers and laity in that state or region be given an opportunity to participate in the decision-making process.

NATIONAL

That each country, where practical, conduct a national assembly, at which consideration would be given to business pertaining to the ministry of the church in that country. Further, that each country determine the frequency, format, and voting constituency of its assembly. All business conducted at any national assembly must be in keeping with the *Minutes* of the International General Assembly. That healing and reconciliation of the races be a priority and that each governing body of each nation reflect the races in its structure.

INTERNATIONAL

1. That the Church of God, in accordance with the Biblical pattern, is an international church. It is international in scope, operation, and ministry, working for a common ministry and purpose in various nations and cultures of the world.
2. That the scope of the church is "all nations," "every creature," and "every kindred, tongue, and people," in obedience to Christ's command to "go into all the world." The church, as a truly international organization, transcends culture, race, nationalism, politics, and economics. Therefore, it considers the world its parish, and all of its constituents are valued and necessary members of one international body.
3. That the Church of God is international in the highest and finest sense, working for a brotherhood among all races, peoples, customs, and nations, which is made possible through a network of offices and personnel on the local, district, state, provincial, and territorial levels. God set the gifts of administration within the church, and these gifts are not restricted in their operation by national boundaries or cultural distinctions.
4. That all of the Biblical ministries were given for all people of the earth. The Great Commission sets forth the international ministry to "preach the gospel to every creature," to make

disciples and teach all nations. To this end the Church of God is dedicated. Further, our first priorities are to love God and love people (Matthew 22:36-40).

CELEBRATING OUR HERITAGE: MISSION-FAITH-IDENTITY CENTENNIAL RESOLUTION (1996)
(66th A., 1996, Item 1, pp. 52-55)

I. IMPLEMENTING OUR MISSION

WHEREAS the Church of God has experienced 100 years of Holy Spirit revival since the outpouring of the Holy Spirit at Shearer Schoolhouse in 1896; and

WHEREAS God has abundantly blessed and prospered the Church of God as evidenced by its growth to over 4 million members and its representation in approximately 130 countries around the world; and

WHEREAS the Great Commission of Jesus Christ to "go into all the world and preach the gospel to every creature" cannot be fulfilled unless believers take the responsibility to be a personal witness,

THEREFORE BE IT RESOLVED that we reaffirm our mission to perpetuate the full gospel of Jesus Christ (Matthew 28:19, 20), in the Spirit and power of Pentecost (Acts 2:1-4, 6, 13-18), through specific attention to and emphasis upon the centrality of God's Word, world evangelization, ministerial development, Christian discipleship, lay ministry, Biblical stewardship, church growth, church planting, family enrichment, and servant leadership; and

BE IT FURTHER RESOLVED that we implement this mission expeditiously, utilizing every available resource, understanding the urgency of the hour and acknowledging our dependence on the power of the Holy Spirit to effectively reach our generation for Christ.

II. REAFFIRMING OUR FAITH

WHEREAS one of the greatest strengths of the Church of God has been and still is our insistence on the authority of Scriptures; and

WHEREAS if we are to perpetuate Pentecost in its purest and most dynamic form, we must do everything we can to preserve its doctrinal integrity; and

WHEREAS the Church of God stands now, as it has always stood, for the whole Bible rightly divided and for the New Testament as the only rule for government and discipline; and

WHEREAS the Church of God has sought from its inception and still seeks to exemplify corporate and individual holiness in the light of Christ's purity and His soon return (1 John 3:1-3); and

WHEREAS the success or failure of this Pentecostal heritage we seek to perpetuate is going to depend on how well we live out the faith we proclaim;

THEREFORE BE IT RESOLVED that we reaffirm our Declaration of Faith as an accurate and effective statement of our theological position; and

BE IT FURTHER RESOLVED that we reaffirm our confidence in our doctrinal and practical commitments as sound, Scripturally based positions, and that we believe these standards are realistic expectations of faith; and

BE IT FURTHER RESOLVED that we reaffirm our holiness/Pentecostal tradition and our fundamental theological heritage as we serve God into the next century.

III. Recognizing Our Identity

WHEREAS the Church of God from its inception has had its own identifying characteristics and was organized to be different from other churches which were perceived to have compromised their Biblical integrity; and

WHEREAS the tendency of individuals, as well as corporate bodies, over a period of time, is to become more like others and to lose their distinctiveness; and

WHEREAS in the midst of the perversity and corruption of the world and the apostasy and compromise that characterizes so much of the modern church, we need to confess our sins, guard against compromise, and pray through in each generation, believing God will cleanse and keep on cleansing us from all sin;

THEREFORE BE IT RESOLVED on this occasion of the centennial celebration of the outpouring of the Holy Spirit at Shearer Schoolhouse, we reaffirm our commitment to those principles upon which the movement was founded and by which it has been guided for 110 years; and

BE IT FURTHER RESOLVED that we reaffirm our uncompromising identity as a Pentecostal church, which still believes in the experience of the baptism in the Holy Spirit with the initial evidence of speaking in other tongues as the Spirit gives the utterance, the manifestation of the fruit of the Spirit in the lives of believers, and the operation of the spiritual gifts in the life of the church; and

BE IT FINALLY RESOLVED that we reaffirm our belief in and our commitment to our historical distinctives. May we forever be known as a church that is Christian, holiness, Pentecostal, evangelistic, benevolent and discipling.

CHURCH GOVERNMENT—
GENERAL
(S1 through S20)

**Portfolio Assignments for the Church of God
International Executive Committee, pages 52-56**
(See S6. International Executive Committee, I.4., p.72)

GENERAL OVERSEER

International Executive Committee
International Executive Council
International Council
General Advisory Council
Administrative Ministries Council
Ex Officio Chairman of Boards and Committees
Oversight of Divisions
World Missions
Oversight of Covenant Ministry Teams
Administrative Staff
PCCNA Representative
International General Assembly Cabinet
Prayer Commission
Church of God Foundation
Legal Services

Portfolio Assignments for the Church of God International Executive Committee, pages 52-56
(See S6. International Executive Committee, I.4., p.72)

Assistant General Overseer
Divisional Director, Care Ministries

Covenant Ministry Team

Credentials

Benevolence

Chaplain's Commission

Ministerial Care

Helping Hands

Ministry to Israel

Ministerial Advocate

Operation Compassion

Peniel Ministries

Widows/Children

**Portfolio Assignments for the Church of God
International Executive Committee, pages 52-56**
(See S6. International Executive Committee, I.4., p.72)

Assistant General Overseer
Divisional Director, World Evangelization

Covenant Ministry Team
Doctrine and Polity
Historical Commission/Church Historian
Mission North America
Canada Vision 20/20
Hispanic Ministries
Intercultural Advancement Ministries
International Revivalist and Urban Ministries
Men and Women of Action
Ministry to the Military
National Evangelists
Romanian Ministries
USA Missions
*Church Planting
*Church Revitalization
*Church Affiliation/Amalgamation

**Portfolio Assignments for the Church of God
International Executive Committee, pages 52-56**
(See S6. International Executive Committee, I.4., p.72)

Assistant General Overseer
Divisional Director, Education

Covenant Ministry Team
General Board of Education
Global Board of Education
International Bible School
Lee University
Ministry Development
Pentecostal Theological Seminary
School of Ministry
USA Hispanic Educational Ministries

**Portfolio Assignments for the Church of God
International Executive Committee, pages 52-56**
(See S6. International Executive Committee, I.4., p.72)

Secretary General
Divisional Director, Discipleship

Covenant Ministry Team
Communications
Public Relations
International General Assembly Cabinet
Youth and Discipleship
Adult Discipleship
Publications
Support Services
Business and Records
Computer Services
Operations and Security
General Board of Trustees
Benefits Board Consultant

S1. GENERAL CHURCH
I. Name of Church
1. Decision harmoniously made, CHURCH OF GOD, 1 Corinthians 1:2; 2 Corinthians 1:1 (2nd A., 1907, Bk. M., p. 22).

2. "We recommend that local churches use the Church of God emblem for identification" (75th A., 2014).

II. Church Teachings
The Church of God stands now, as it has always stood, for the whole Bible rightly divided, and for the New Testament as the only rule for government and discipline. It has been necessary at times for the International General Assembly of the church to search the Scriptures and interpret the meaning of the Bible to arrive at what is the true and proper teaching of the church on various subjects, but always with the purpose and intention to base our teachings strictly upon the Bible.

III. Form of Government
A. Governing Body
After due consideration the Assembly adopted the following: we do not consider ourselves a legislative or executive body, but judicial only (1st A., 1906, Bk. M., p. 15).

This is understood to mean that we acknowledge Jesus Christ as the Head of the Church (Ephesians 1:22-23; 4:15; Colossians 1:18), and that He guides the church through His Word (2 Timothy 3:16-17) and by His Spirit (John 16:13; Revelation 2:7, 11, 17, 29; 3:6, 13, 22). Therefore, the International General Assembly is to seek to correctly discern the Scriptures by the guidance of the Holy Spirit in regard to doctrine, discipline, church order, and governance (75th A., 2014).

B. Church and State
1. The Church of God is opposed to the union of church and state under any circumstances (3rd A., 1908, Bk. M., p. 27).

2. The Church of God is definitely opposed to any form of dictatorship in matters pertaining to state and civil government. We heartily endorse the democratic way of life and faithfully pledge ourselves to its support, maintenance, and progress (37th A., 1942, p. 36)

3. We, the Church of God resolve that, it is not the right of governments to compel churches or church related institutions to participate in or fund activities that are morally reprehensible (74th A., 2012).

C. **Local Church Part of the Assembly**

1. The local churches, the names of which are officially registered with the Church of God, Cleveland, Tennessee, U.S.A., are the result of the faithful services of the ministers and representatives of the International General Assembly, and these churches, when thus received by the representatives of the International General Assembly, then became and composed a part of the International General Assembly (15th A., 1920, p. 50; 45th A., 1954, pp. 27, 28; 50th A., 1964, p. 54; [1994]).

All Church of God congregations, which are officially registered with the Church of God, Cleveland, Tennessee, USA, are part of the International General Assembly. Further, the right of any amalgamated church as a whole, to withdraw from the International General Assembly is not recognized and does not exist. Those members of a local church who prove disloyal to the government and teachings of the Church of God as determined by the International General Assembly or who are otherwise disorderly are to be dealt with as individuals (75th A., 2014).

2. If a church is organized and they do not accept the teachings of the Assembly, they cannot be recognized by headquarters [at any level of church government] as a Church of God (15th A., 1920, p. 68).

D. **Incorporation of Churches** (44th A., 1952, p. 30; 68th A., 2000, pp. 82, 83)

State/territorial overseers, on behalf of the churches under their oversight, are encouraged to investigate the necessity of incorporation, under various state laws, after legal advice from competent local attorneys.

It is understood that the laws of some states may prefer incorporation of local churches, while the laws of other states may not. Forms for articles of incorporation, charters, and bylaws of incorporations of local Churches of God shall be prepared, and all of such documents shall be approved by the International Executive Committee in consultation with the Church of God legal counsel, in accordance with all aspects of Church of God polity. All of such documents shall contain provisions that incorporated local churches shall be subject to the Church of God General Assembly *Minutes* in all pertinent matters, including conformity with Church of God deed and property requirements.

(See S57. INCORPORATION OF LOCAL CHURCHES.)

BOOK OF DISCIPLINE, CHURCH ORDER, AND GOVERNANCE 59

E. **Reception of Churches or Association of Churches** (63rd A., 1990, p. 78)

When a church or association of churches desires to become affiliated with the Church of God, thus becoming part of the International General Assembly, the church or association must follow the established procedure for acceptance into the Church of God as set forth by the International General Assembly. Appropriate forms of organization, with resolutions to unite with the church, must be processed in a legal business meeting to show acceptance of the faith, government, polity, and practices of the Church of God, and the willingness to abide by the actions of the International General Assembly.

(See S60. AFFILIATION WITH CHURCH OF GOD.)

S2. BYLAWS OF THE CHURCH OF GOD
(53rd A., 1970, p. 27, 28; 67th A., 1998, p. 54; 68th A., 2000, pp. 83-86)

ARTICLE I
Name

The official name shall be Church of God (1 Corinthians 1:2; 2 Corinthians 1: 1).

ARTICLE II
Temporal Nature

The Church of God is incorporated in the state of Tennessee (U.S.A.) as a not-for-profit organization and is recognized as a 501 (c) (3) corporation under the Internal Revenue Code (U.S.A.) or the corresponding sections of any prior or future Internal Revenue Code (U.S.A.).

ARTICLE III
Governance

The current edition of the *Minutes* of the Church of God International General Assembly contains rulings of the most recent meeting of the Church of God International General Assembly, and church polity statements and rules of church discipline, order, and governance still in effect from all previous Church of God General Assemblies, including these bylaws.

ARTICLE IV
Mission Statement

The mission of the Church of God is to communicate the full gospel of Jesus Christ (Matthew 28:19, 20) in the Spirit and power of Pentecost (Acts 2:1-4, 6, 13-18) (71st A., 2006, p. 44).

ARTICLE V
Members

The membership of the Church of God shall be composed of Christians who have accepted the teachings, doctrines, and government of the Church of God, and who have been formally received into its fellowship pursuant to the guidelines established by the International General Assembly. Procedures for excluding members shall be set by the International General Assembly upon recommendation of the International General Council.

ARTICLE VI
Governing Bodies

1. INTERNATIONAL GENERAL ASSEMBLY

Members

The International General Assembly is composed of all members and ministers of the Church of God 16 years of age and above. Members and ministers of the Church of God present and registered at the International General Assembly shall comprise its voting constituency (64th A., 1992, p. 73; 65th A., 1994, Item 1, p. 78).

Purpose

The purpose of the International General Assembly is to advance the mission, vision, and commitments of the Church of God as stated in the International General Assembly *Minutes* (73rd A., 2010).

Meeting

The International General Assembly shall meet biennially to consider all recommendations from the International General Council.

Parliamentary Authority

Robert's Rules of Order Newly Revised shall serve as the official guide for the business of the International General Assembly in all matters to which they are applicable and in which they are not inconsistent with the bylaws of the International General Assembly.

Elections

The International General Assembly shall elect the general overseer, the assistant general overseers, the secretary general, the director of Youth and Discipleship, the assistant director of Youth and Discipleship, the director of World Missions, and the assistant director of World Missions (58th A., 1980, pp. 29-32, (1-4; 73rd A., 2010).

Officers, Committees

The officers of the International General Assembly shall consist of the moderator and a secretary. The general overseer shall preside as moderator. He shall also appoint parliamentarians to serve during the International General Assembly meetings. He shall also appoint members of committees called for by the International General Assembly.

The secretary general shall serve the Assembly as secretary. He shall be responsible for recording actions by the Assembly and shall be the custodian of the records of the Assembly.

Parliamentary Procedure

Debate on all motions shall be governed by the current edition of *Robert's Rules of Order Newly Revised*. Each member has the right to speak on every question. However, he cannot make a second speech on the same question as long as any member who has not spoken on the question desires the floor (*Robert's Rules of Order Newly Revised*). It is the prerogative of the moderator to recognize each speaker and to determine a balance of negative and affirmative speeches.

Debate may be limited by a proper motion (*Robert's Rules of Order Newly Revised*).

2. INTERNATIONAL GENERAL COUNCIL

Members

The International General Council is composed of all ordained bishops of the Church of God, who shall comprise its voting constituency.

Agenda

1. The International General Council shall meet biennially to consider all recommendations from the International Executive Council. The International General Council agenda shall be made available by the most efficient and effective methods to the ordained bishops at least thirty (30) days prior to the International General Council (75th A., 2014).

2. The International General Council shall consider and prepare such recommendations as are Scriptural and proper in matters pertaining to the welfare of the church. Such recommendations are to be presented to the International General Assembly for final disposition.

3. The current edition of *Robert's Rules of Order Newly Revised* shall serve as the official guide for the business of the International General Council in all matters to which they are applicable and in which they are not inconsistent with the bylaws of the International General Council. As a guide for the order of business, the agenda presented by the International Executive Council shall claim the attention of the Council first.

4. Any new business shall be presented to the chairman of the motions committee, which committee shall receive, classify, clarify, eliminate duplication, and dispatch for placement on the agenda following the completion of the printed agenda. Any new business presented to the motions committee shall be presented in typewritten form not later than 2 p.m. of the third day of the International General Council.

5. The International General Council shall nominate to the International General Assembly the general overseer, the assistant general overseers, the secretary general, the general Youth and Discipleship director, the assistant general Youth and Discipleship director, the director of World Missions, and the assistant director of World Missions (73rd A., 2010 [effective 2012]).

6. The International General Council shall elect the Council of Eighteen ([1972]; 58th A., 1980, pp. 29-32 (1-4).

Officers and Committees

1. The officers of the International General Council shall consist of the moderator and a secretary. The general overseer shall preside as moderator. He shall also appoint parliamentarians to serve during the International General Council meetings. He shall also appoint members of committees called for by the International General Council.

2. The secretary general shall serve the Council as secretary. He shall be responsible for recording actions by the Council and shall be the custodian of the records of the Council.

Parliamentary Procedure and Authority

1. The names of all persons on the nomination ballots receiving twenty-five (25) or less votes for an elected office shall be posted in an appropriate designated place in lieu of reading those names to the International General Council.

2. Debate on all motions shall be governed by the current edition of *Robert's Rules of Order Newly Revised*. Each member has the right to

speak on every question. However, he cannot make a second speech on the same question as long as any member who has not spoken on the question desires the floor (*Robert's Rules of Order Newly Revised*). It is the prerogative of the moderator to recognize each speaker and to determine a balance of negative and affirmative speeches.

3. Debate may be limited by a proper motion (*Robert's Rules of Order Newly Revised*).

3. INTERNATIONAL EXECUTIVE COUNCIL

Authority

This council shall consider and act upon any and all matters pertaining to the general interest and welfare of the Church of God.

Members

The general overseer, his assistants, the secretary general, and eighteen councilors [the Council of Eighteen] elected by the International General Council shall constitute the International Executive Council of the church.

Meeting

At a time set by the general overseer, the International Executive Council shall meet and adopt recommendations to be brought before the International General Council.

Duties and Responsibilities

The duties and responsibilities of the International Executive Council shall be set by the International General Assembly upon recommendation by the International General Council.

ARTICLE VII
Executive Board

International Executive Committee—The executive officers of the Church of God shall be the general overseer, three assistant general overseers, and the secretary general. These shall constitute the International Executive Committee. Their tenure in office, manner of selection, duties and authorities, and procedure for filling vacancies shall be decided by the International General Assembly upon recommendation from the International General Council.

ARTICLE VIII
Committees

Standing Boards and Committees—Standing boards and committees as called for by the International General Assembly or International General Council shall be appointed by the International

Executive Committee. The general overseer shall be an *ex officio* member of all standing boards and committees.

ARTICLE IX
Parliamentary Authority

The latest edition of *Robert's Rules of Order Newly Revised* shall serve as the official parliamentary guide for conducting the business of the church.

ARTICLE X
Amendment of Bylaws
Amendment

The power to alter, amend, or repeal these bylaws shall be vested in the International General Assembly and exercised only by a two-thirds vote of the International General Assembly upon recommendation of a two-thirds vote of the International General Council.

Previous Notice

In order to amend, alter or repeal these bylaws, previous notice will be considered fulfilled if the following guidelines to notify the constituency are observed:

(1) That previous notice items be made available by the most efficient and effective methods to ministers who report to the Church of God International Offices in Cleveland, Tennessee, U.S.A., including national and territorial leaders, the notice and copies of the proposed change(s) to the Bylaws of the Church of God to be considered by the International General Council, not later than 90 days prior to the opening of the International General Council. Pastors should make this notice available by public announcement and/or posting to their congregations (75th A., 2014).

(2) Include the notice and a copy of the proposed change(s) to the Bylaws of the Church of God to be considered by the International General Council in at least two issues of the *Church of God Evangel* preceding the opening of the International General Council.

(3) Post the notice and a copy of the proposed change(s) on the church's Internet web site.

(4) The proposed change(s) may be amended, but cannot be amended beyond the scope of the notice. Any change of the bylaws approved by the International General Assembly will go into effect

immediately upon its adoption, unless the motion to adopt specifies another time for its becoming effective.

S3. INTERNATIONAL GENERAL ASSEMBLY

I. DEFINITION (15th A., 1920, p. 50 (2); [1994]; 68th A., 2000, pp. 78, 86, 87)

1. The International General Assembly of the Church of God (Cleveland, Tennessee, U.S.A.) is that organized body with full power and authority to designate the teaching, government, principles, and practices of all the local churches composing said Assembly [1994]).

2. One of the first principles accepted in the earliest history of its organization was that we accept the whole Bible rightly divided, which is today one of the most sacred principles. From its earliest history, the Church of God has been guided by the sole authority of Holy Scripture; therefore, we meet in biennial conference with all ministers and laity who wish to attend to search the Scriptures and put them into practice. All the changes in government and polity have been duly authorized by the International General Assembly in its various sessions which adopts measures by a majority vote of all Church of God members present and registered at the International General Assembly. Nominees by the International General Council are declared elected to office on a majority vote of the International General Assembly. (15th A., 1920; 45th A., 1954, p. 33; 64th A., 1992, p. 73; 75th A., 2014).

II. PROCEDURES

1. The question as to whether records should be kept of this and other Assemblies like this was discussed, passed, and recommended as Scriptural (1st A., 1906, Bk. M., p. 15).

2. Arrangements for the time and place of the International General Assembly shall be left to the International Executive Council (35th A., 1940, p. 31).

3. The general overseer is authorized to call an International General Assembly of ministers provided that travel and other conditions are such that the International Executive Committee and the Council of Eighteen deem it wise to do so (40th A., 1945, p. 31).

III. ROLE OF THE LAITY IN THE INTERNATIONAL GENERAL ASSEMBLY (66th A., 1996, Item. 7, p. 62, 63)

Whereas New Testament church lay leaders were partners in ministry and in discerning major decisions affecting the church in general (Acts 6:1-7; 15:2, 4, 22, 30; Romans 16:1-15; 1 Corinthians 16:1-3, 15-19; 2 Corinthians 8:18, 19; Philippians 4:1-3; Colossians 4:7-17); and

Since the first General Assembly in 1906, it has been the practice of the Church of God to rely on this vital partnership between laity and ministers; and

The International General Assembly grants to its laity the same voice that it affords all credentialed ministers during the International General Assembly sessions,

Therefore, when funds are available, after the pastoral family's needs have been met, churches are encouraged to provide financial assistance for laity to attend the International General Assembly and national convention; and

All delegates (preregistered at least 30 days in advance of the Assembly), shall receive by the most efficient and effective methods a copy of agenda items that are being presented to the International General Council for possible inclusion on the International General Assembly agenda (75th A., 2014); and

Study shall be given by the International Executive Council to increasing the time allotted for International General Assembly business, to provide more opportunity for laity to participate in the discussion of the issues; and

We affirm the Biblical and historical role and importance of the laity in the International General Assembly of the Church of God.

S4. INTERNATIONAL GENERAL COUNCIL

I. SELECTION (45th A., 1954, p. 33; 68th A., 2000, pp. 78, 81)

The International General Council is composed of all ordained bishops and shall comprise its voting ranks. Ordained ministers, exhorters, and laity shall be privileged to sit in the International General Council, without voting privileges (51st A., 1966, p. 19).

II. DUTIES

The International General Council shall:

1. Meet biennially to consider and prepare such recommendations as are Scriptural and proper in all matters pertaining to the welfare of the church. Such recommendations are to be presented to the International General Assembly for final disposition.

2. Nominate to the International General Assembly the general overseer, his assistants, the secretary general, the general Youth and Discipleship director, the assistant general Youth and Discipleship

director, the director of World Missions, and the assistant director of World Missions (49th A., 1962, p. 31; 52nd A., 1968, pp. 33, 34 (1); (1972); 58th A., 1980, pp. 29-32 Items 1- 3; 73rd A., 2010 [effective 2012]).

3. Elect the members of the Council of Eighteen (61 A., 1986, p. 53 (1).

III. INTERNATIONAL GENERAL COUNCIL AGENDA

Inasmuch as the official agenda, which is to claim the attention of the International General Council, is made available by the most efficient and effective methods to the ordained bishops at least thirty (30) days prior to the opening of the International General Council, all recommendations must be received by the International Executive Council in time for consideration at its April session in order to appear on the International General Council agenda (53rd A., 1970, p. 57 Item 18, 75th A., 2014).

To allow opportunity for consideration and perfection, all resolutions prepared by the duly appointed Resolutions Committee, shall be distributed by the best available means to all present ordained bishops at or before the time of adjournment of the last business session on the day before they are to be considered by the International General Council (75th A., 2014).

IV. INTERNATIONAL GENERAL COUNCIL MOTIONS COMMITTEE

All new motions and resolutions that are to claim the attention of the International General Council shall be written and given a place on the agenda, and to serve this purpose we recommend the appointment, by the chair, of a motions committee of five, who shall receive, classify, and place on the agenda such motions and resolutions. (This committee is to function during the time that the International General Council is in session) (46th A., 1956, p. 22, 75th A., 2014).

Previous notice shall be required for any motion which greatly alters the organizational structure of the Church of God. When motions are presented to the Motions Committee, the following guidelines will be followed:

1. Each motion will be processed by the Motions Committee according to the guidelines of the Church of God book of *Minutes*.

2. The Motions Committee will initially determine if the motion would "greatly alter the organizational structure of the Church of God."

3. If, in the opinion of the moderator, the motion would "greatly alter the organizational structure of the Church of God,"

the motion will be read to the body by the chairman of the Motions Committee at the direction of the moderator with the notation that it is a motion that will require previous notice before final disposition.

4. The moderator will explain that if the motion passes in the present International General Council, it will be placed on the agenda of the following International General Council in order to fulfill the requirement of previous notice.

5. The item will then be open for full debate on the presently-convening International General Council floor.

6. If the motion does not receive a majority vote, it falls to the floor.

7. If the motion receives a majority vote, it is committed to the International Executive Council with the mandate that it be placed on the agenda for the next International General Council in a manner that fulfills the requirements of previous notice (74th A., 2012).

S5. INTERNATIONAL EXECUTIVE COUNCIL
(LAMA, p. 555; 25th A., 1930, p. 23 (20); 37th A., 1942, p. 36 (1); 39th A., 1944, p. 37 (23); 43rd A., 1950, pp. 14, 15 (5); 45th A., 1954, p. 34 (34); 50th A., 1964, p. 50 (5); 50th A., 1964, p. 56 (19); 52nd A., 1968, p. 33, 34 (1); 61st A., 1986, p. 53 (1); 62nd A., 1988, Journal, p. 52; 64th A., 1992, pp. 87, 88; 65th A., 1994, Item 8, p. 89; 68th A., 2000, pp. 77, 78; 69th A., 2002, p. 50; 71st A., 2006, pp. 46, 47; 73rd A., 2010: 75th A., 2014; 77th A., 2018).

I. SELECTION

1. The general overseer, his assistants, the secretary general, and eighteen councilors [the Council of Eighteen] constitute the International Executive Council of the church.

2. The International Executive Council is comprised of the International Executive Committee and eighteen (18) elected members. Not less than twelve (12) members shall be pastors at the time of their election. Further, three (3) members of the Council of Eighteen shall be at the time of their election foreign nationals residing and ministering outside the United States (69th A., 2002, p. 50). No member of the International Executive Committee who has just completed his tenure of office shall be eligible to serve on the International Executive Council for the ensuing International General Assembly term (77th A., 2018).

3. In accordance with the memorandum of agreement, the moderator of the Full Gospel Church of God in South Africa shall be a member of the International Executive Council of the Church of God in America, and the general overseer of the Church of God shall

be a member of the Executive Council of the Full Gospel Church of God in South Africa (46A., 1956, p. 28 (47)).

4. The eighteen (18) members shall be elected by the International General Council biennially, with a member being eligible to succeed himself for one term (S3, V, A, 9).

5. The eighteen (18) members shall be elected from the ordained bishops and no chief executive officer, or his assistant, of any church agency which presents a budget to a divisional leader, shall be eligible to serve on the International Executive Council.

II. Procedure for Filling Vacancies

Should any one of the 18 positions on the Council of Eighteen be vacated because of death, disability, advancement, resignation, or the member in any wise being disqualified, the General Overseer shall submit to the International Executive Council, in session, the names of the next two men receiving the highest votes on previous ballots who are eligible at the time of this special election, and whose election would retain the required minimum numbers of pastors and/or foreign nationals as required by the International General Assembly *Minutes*. The one receiving the majority vote of the International Executive Council shall be declared elected to fill the unexpired term. If more than one half of the vacated term remains, the member elected to fill that term will be eligible to succeed himself for only one additional term. If a vacancy occurs after April 1 of an International General Assembly year, that vacancy will not be filled (71st A., 2006, pp. 46, 47).

III. Duties and Authorities

1. This council shall consider and act upon any and all matters pertaining to the general interest and welfare of the Church of God. At a time set by the general overseer, the said council shall meet and adopt recommendations to be brought before the International General Council (56th A., 1976, p. 49, 1, 2).

2. All measures designed to change or alter any teaching of the Church of God, before being presented to the International General Council, shall first be submitted to the International Executive Council in writing prior to the meeting of the International General Council (45th A., 1954, p. 34 (34); 49th A., 1962, p. 34 (11)).

3. All measures designed to change, alter, or delete any doctrine of the Church of God as prescribed in the Declaration of Faith, before

being presented to the International General Assembly, shall be first submitted to the International Executive Council in writing twelve (12) months prior to the regular session of the International General Council, and must have a three-fourths majority vote to carry. The measure shall then be submitted to the International General Council for consideration, and if the International General Council approves the measure by a three-fourths vote, the International Executive Committee shall publicize the said measure by all means deemed appropriate, thus giving the membership an opportunity to consider and vote on the said measure in the International General Assembly before it becomes a ruling (45th A., 1954, p. 34 (34); 49th A., 1962, p. 34 (11); 50th A., 1964, p. 50 (5); p. 56 (19); 75th A., 2014).

4. All motions offered to the International Executive Council for consideration to be included on the agenda for the International General Assembly, and/or to be included on the agenda for the International General Council, shall be published online via the ministerial reporting website at the end of each International Executive Council meeting (74th A., 2012).

All business before the International Executive Council between assemblies, concluded and decided, be made available to all credentialed ministers through the ministerial reporting website. Any disciplinary actions will not be included (75th A., 2014).

5. The distribution of tithes sent to the international offices of the church shall be in the hands of the general overseer and the International Executive Council (13th A., 1917, pp. 33, 40; 26th A., 1931, p. 104 (2); 33rd A., 1938, p. 51 (4); 39th A., 1944, p. 38 (1); 42nd A., 1948, p. 29; 50th A., 1964, p. 50 (5); p. 56 (19).

6. Matters which concern difficulties or measures relating to one or more of the general officials shall be referred to the Council of Eighteen for decision (see **S6. V. Discipline**).

7. Its duty shall be to counsel with the general overseer in all matters pertaining to the general interest of the church. This body of men, or a majority of the same, shall have power to estop any general official of the Church of God for any misconduct, until proper procedures have been followed (64th. A., 1992, p. 87).

8. The general overseer, with the International Executive Council, be authorized to give one of his assistants the World Missions portfolio and assign his duties and authorities (52nd A., 1968; 77th A., 2018).

9. The International Executive Council shall meet every two years with the International Council to discuss and project international ministries (Proverbs 11:14) (59th A., 1982, p. 32).

10. Allotments for aged and disabled ministers shall be determined by the International Executive Council.

11. Ministers' credentials having been revoked for the cause of improper conduct with the opposite sex, shall not be restored to them until approved by a three-fourths majority vote of the International Executive Council (42nd A., 1948, p. 29; 65th A., 1994, Item 16, p. 91).

12. The International Executive Council is authorized to reorganize, amplify, and clarify as necessary all information in the International General Assembly *Minutes* pertaining to property ownership and the various boards of trustees. It is understood that no changes will be made in the intent of the measures, only rearrangement and updating. Further, the International Executive Council shall make this material in its reorganized form available to every pastor and ordained bishop as soon as possible following the International General Assembly (65th A., 1994, Item 8, p. 89).

13. Whereas the Church of God is an international church serving in many nations, societies and cultures; and words may not always convey the same meaning nor the same level of social and cultural appropriateness in these various settings,

Therefore the International Executive Council is authorized to reword information in the International General Assembly *Minutes* to clarify its meaning and protect its social and cultural appropriateness. It is understood that no changes will be made in the intent or essence of the measures.

Further, the International Executive Council is authorized to commission the preparation of an international version of the International General Assembly *Minutes* that takes into consideration the differences in laws and customs between the United States of America and other countries (67th A., 1998, pp. 52, 53).

14. The initial structure of a U.S.A. National Council/Assembly shall be the same as the International General Council/Assembly, and that the International Executive Council shall schedule time for business unique to the United States of America to be handled during the week of the International General Assembly (71st A., 2006, pp. 46, 47).

15. The International Executive Council is tasked with the responsibility of actualizing a global context of ministry to include, but not limited to, enhancing the availability of language-specific resources; recognition and utilization of international leaders during general church events, refining programs, methods, and systems to reflect the international nature of the church; and challenging the church to think globally (77th A., 2018).

S6. INTERNATIONAL EXECUTIVE COMMITTEE
(39th A., 1944 p. 30; 40th A., 1945, p. 28; 44th A., 1952 pp. 31, 35; 45th A., 1954, p. 30; 50th A., 1964 pp. 50, 51; 52nd A., 1968, pp. 33, 34; 64th A., 1992, pp. 86, 87; 68th A., 2000, p. 78)

I. OFFICES-PORTFOLIOS-ORGANIZATION

1. The following offices shall constitute the International Executive Committee: general overseer, first assistant general overseer, second assistant general overseer, third assistant general overseer, secretary general.

2. The general overseer, the three assistants, and the secretary general shall compose the International Executive Committee. We further recommend that the general overseer, with the International Executive Council, designate the fields of their activities.

3. Executive portfolios are to be assigned at the first business session following the election of the officers and are subject to periodic review by the International Executive Council.

4. The executive portfolios assigned by the General Overseer and the International Executive Council for the current Assembly period are listed on pages 52-56 in this book of *Minutes*. (60th A., 1984, p. 41; 69th A., 2002, p. 49).

II. FILLING VACATED OFFICES

Should the offices of any two or more members of the International Executive Committee be vacated simultaneously through death, accident, national disaster, war, national epidemic, or otherwise, a call shall be issued within thirty (30) days by the remaining members of the International Executive Committee for an emergency meeting of the ministers of the Church of God. Three members of the International Executive Council may, by petition, call an emergency meeting of the ministers. The ordained bishops shall nominate to this special session of the ministers names to fill the offices thus vacated. In this special session the ministers shall elect the members to fill the unexpired terms of office (50th A., 1964, p. 52).

III. Duties and Authorities

The International Executive Committee shall:

1. Appoint all state and provincial overseers (35th A., 1940, p. 31).

2. Be authorized to permit state overseers in mission states to continue their work, when necessary, beyond the usual tenure limitation. Further, that time served as a state overseer in mission territory not be counted as part of the tenure limitation on an overseer, if he is appointed to serve as state overseer of a non-mission state (45th A., 1954 p. 26).

3. Appoint all general standing boards and committees. When an individual is appointed as an Administrative Bishop and then elected to the Council of Eighteen, he is not to be appointed to a standing board (70th A., 2004 p. 57).

4. Appoint the presidents of church colleges.

5. Appoint boards to hear cases of appeals of ministers.

6. Act as an emergency board.

7. In case of an emergency the International Executive Committee, with the consent of the respective Ministry heads, shall have authority to transfer money, temporarily, from one Ministry to another (35th A., 1940, p. 31).

8. After a member of the International Executive Committee has served eight years, he shall be ineligible to serve in that capacity for a period of two years (45th A., 1954, p. 27).

9. The appointments of all personnel made by all standing boards and committees and all salaries of same, shall be made subject to the approval of the International Executive Committee (46th A., 1956, p. 28).

10. The International Executive Committee is empowered to counsel with the ministers of any state through the offices of the state overseer and State Council with reference to any change in the state that is deemed advisable to properly carry out an effective operational program, subject to the ratification of the ministers in the respective state (51st A., 1966, p. 59).

11. That a Generational Task Force be established to identify and embrace the differing requirements of generational ministry. The Generational Task Force will be appointed by the International Executive Committee and will meet at least yearly to provide input to the International Executive Committee regarding the needs of the various generations (77th A., 2018).

IV. LOCAL CHURCH DEVELOPMENT PLAN (72nd A., 2008)

A Local Church Development Plan shall be implemented by the International Executive Committee, in conjunction with each respective state/regional overseer, for the purpose of increasing the effectiveness of local churches in the fulfillment of their mission, through a plan designed to involve lay leadership, together with pastoral oversight, for church growth in the twenty-first century.

This shall be a standardized plan designed to meet the needs of local churches at each numerical level (see S47).

V. DISCIPLINE (64th A., 1992, pp. 86, 87)

1. Procedures concerning an International Executive Committee member who has been accused of any misconduct shall become the responsibility of the Council of Eighteen, called into executive session and moderated [chaired] by the first elected member.

2. If the Council of Eighteen believes there is reason to do so, an investigative committee shall be selected from the Council to inquire into any formal charges of misconduct.

3. The Council of Eighteen shall then consider the findings of the investigative committee.

4. Once charges have been filed, the said International Executive Committee member shall be relieved of all responsibilities but retain his salary and benefits until the matter has been resolved.

5. If the Council of Eighteen agrees that the findings of the investigative committee warrant charges being filed, a trial board shall be appointed by the Council to hear the charges.

6. Any appeal of the decision of the trial board must be presented to the chairman [the first elected member, serving as moderator] of the Council of Eighteen, in writing, within 10 days of receiving the written notification of the trial board's decision.

7. If granted by a majority vote of the Council of Eighteen, a board of appeal shall be appointed by the Council. Members of the investigative committee and trial boards shall be ineligible to serve.

8. If the appeal board sustains the guilty verdict, the member shall be removed from office immediately and the filling of the vacancy shall proceed as provided for in the International General Assembly *Minutes*.

9. If the offense warrants such action, the chairman of the Council of Eighteen shall notify the respective state overseer to sign the termination of credentials form.

S7. GENERAL OVERSEER (Presiding Bishop, see p. 104.)

I. Selection

1. The general overseer shall be nominated by the International General Council and elected by the International General Assembly. He shall be the highest officer of the church, and it shall be his duty to have general supervision of the work in all fields (39th A., 1944, p. 37).

2. He shall be elected for a four-year term, and he shall be eligible to serve no more than eight consecutive years in this office or on the Executive Committee (41st A., 1946, p. 26; 73rd A., 2010).

II. Duties and Authorities

The general overseer shall:

1. Act as chairman or moderator of the International General Assembly, the International General Council, and the International Executive Council (39th A., 1944, p. 36; 43rd A., 1950, p. 15).

2. Sign and issue credentials to ministers.

3. Keep a record of all the ministers within the bounds of the International General Assembly.

4. Look after the general interest of the churches.

5. Together with the International Executive Council, be authorized to give one of his assistants the World Missions portfolio and assign his duties and authorities (52nd A., 1968; 77th A., 2018).

6. Together with his assistants and the secretary general, appoint all general standing boards and committees biennially, said appointments to be made within two weeks of the close of the International General Assembly, except in cases of emergency (Amended 50th A., 1964, p. 56; 52nd A., 1968, p. 34; 73rd A., 2010).

When an individual is appointed as an Administrative Bishop and then elected to the Council of Eighteen, he is not to be appointed to a standing board (70th A., 2004 p. 57).

7. Together with his assistants and the secretary general, appoint all state and provincial overseers biennially and to have jurisdiction over them (50th A., 1964 p. 56; 52nd A., 1968, p. 33).

8. Together with the other members of the International Executive Committee, to dismiss any appointee in case of necessity.

9. In the event of any emergency which warrants doing so, call the Council of Eighteen and associate councilors into session for counsel.

10. Call the International Executive Council or the International General Council into session.

11. The ministerial authority of no person shall be finally terminated until a revocation of his ministry be approved and signed by the general overseer and the chief executive officer of the church in the state or territory in whose jurisdiction the case may be (43rd A., 1950, p. 15).

III. PROCEDURE FOR FILLING VACANCY

In case the office of the general overseer be vacated because of death, disability, or the incumbent in any wise being disqualified, the first assistant general overseer shall fill the unexpired term of the general overseer (50th A., 1964, pp. 51, 52).

S8. ASSISTANT GENERAL OVERSEERS
(Executive Bishops, see p. 104.)

(23rd A., 1928, p. 25; 32nd A., 1937, p. 36; 39th A, 1944 p. 37; 40th A., 1945, p. 28; 41st A., 1946, p. 26; 44th A., 1952, p. 31; 48th A, 1960, p. 32; 50th A., 1964, p. 50; 73rd A., 2010).

I. SELECTION

1. The International General Assembly has created the offices of first, second, and third assistant general overseers. The duties of the first, second, and third assistant general overseers shall be to assist the general overseer.

2. The assistant general overseers shall be nominated by the International General Council and elected by the International General Assembly.

3. The assistant general overseers shall be elected for a four-year term, and they shall be eligible to serve no more than eight consecutive years in either of said offices or on the International Executive Committee.

II. DUTIES AND AUTHORITIES

The assistant general overseers shall devote their entire time to the general interest of the church (32nd A., 1937, p. 36).

III. PROCEDURE FOR FILLING VACANCY

Should the office of an assistant general overseer be vacated because of advancement, death, disability, or the incumbent in any wise being disqualified, the remaining International Executive Committee members shall automatically advance in the order of their election by the International General Assembly (73rd A., 2010).

S9. SECRETARY GENERAL (Executive Bishop, see p. 104.)

(68th A., 2000, pp. 86, 87)

I. SELECTION

1. The secretary general shall be nominated by the International General Council and elected by the International General Assembly.

2. The secretary general shall be elected for a four-year term, and he shall be eligible to serve no more than eight consecutive years in this office or on the International Executive Committee (41st A., 1946, p. 26; 73rd A., 2010).

II. DUTIES AND AUTHORITIES

The secretary general shall:

1. Keep all records and reports of the ministers and churches coming to the international offices of the church (42nd A., 1948, p. 29).

2. Be custodian of all general church records and legal documents.

3. Furnish such reports as the divisional directors of ministries and the International Executive Council may require (73rd A., 2010).

4. Have an audit of financial records and furnish the International General Assembly a statement of all receipts and disbursements, assets and liabilities, such statements to be prepared by a certified public accountant annually (40th A., 1945, p. 177).

III. PROCEDURE FOR FILLING VACANCY

In the event the office of the secretary general be vacated because of death, disability, advancement, or the incumbent in any wise being disqualified, the general overseer shall submit by mail the names of the next two men receiving the highest vote, who were not elected to any general office, to the ordained bishops. The ordained bishops shall select the one who will fill the vacancy in the secretary general's office. Ballots must be returned to the general overseer within twenty (20) days to be valid votes. The one receiving the majority vote shall be declared elected to fill the unexpired term of the secretary general (39th A., 1944, p. 38; 41st A., 1946, p. 22; [1960]; 50th A., 1964, p. 51, Item 6).

S10. MINISTRY OF YOUTH AND DISCIPLESHIP
(42nd A., 1948, p. 33; 46th A., 1956, p. 28; 52nd A., 1968, p. 36; 53rd A., 1970, pp. 40, 41; [1972] [1974]; 73rd A., 2010)

I. DIRECTOR OF YOUTH AND DISCIPLESHIP
(41st A., 1946, p. 22; 42nd. A., 1948, p. 30; 44th A., 1952, p. 30; 46th A., 1956, p. 28, Item 51; 52nd A, 1968, p. 36, Item 4; 53rd A., 1970, pp. 40, 41, Item 8; [1972] [1974]; 73rd A., 2010; 75th A., 2014)

A. Selection, Tenure, and Salary

1. The office of the director of Youth and Discipleship shall be filled by one who shall devote his full time to the promotion of the Church of God youth and discipleship work. He shall be nominated by the International General Council and elected quadrennially (4-year term) by the International General Assembly. He shall not be able to succeed himself beyond one four-year term (effective 2016).

2. The salary of the director of Youth and Discipleship shall be set by the International Executive Council (50th A., 1964, p. 56).

B. Duties and Authorities

The director of Youth and Discipleship shall:

1. Promote the general interest of Youth and Discipleship ministries.

2. Work with the International Executive Committee in arranging for and the promotion of national or regional Youth and Discipleship Conferences, as outlined by the International General Assembly.

3. Cooperate with the general director of Publications in the promotion of all youth and Christian education publications.

4. Plan for and promote the general interest of the Home for Children (51st A., 1966, p. 56).

II. ASSISTANT DIRECTOR OF YOUTH AND DISCIPLESHIP
(49th A., 1962, p. 31; 52nd A., 1968, p. 36; 53rd A., 1970, pp. 40, 41; [1972]; 73rd A., 2010, 75th A., 2014)

A. Selection, Tenure, and Salary

1. The assistant director of Youth and Discipleship shall be nominated by the International General Council and elected quadrennially (4-year term) by the International General Assembly. He shall not be able to succeed himself beyond one four-year term (effective 2016).

2. The salary of the assistant director of Youth and Discipleship shall be set by the International Executive Council (50th A., 1964, p. 56).

B. Duties and Authorities
The assistant director of Youth and Discipleship shall assist the director of Youth and Discipleship.

S11. MINISTRY OF USA MISSIONS (73rd A., 2010)
I. USA MISSIONS BOARD
A. Selection
The USA Missions Board shall consist of not less than five members who shall be appointed biennially by the International Executive Committee (74th A., 2012).

B. Duties and Authorities
The USA Missions Board shall:

1. Serve the needs of the church as they relate to all phases of evangelism and USA missions.

2. Formulate plans and recommendations related to evangelism and church planting. Provide new and practical helps for a vigorous pursuit of a Biblical and balanced evangelistic emphasis.

3. Develop resources suitable for special fields. Offer encouragement for work among all racial and social communities of the nation.

II. RESOLUTION ON USA MISSIONS (70th A., 2004, p. 55; 73rd A., 2010)

WHEREAS most statistical surveys list the U.S.A. as having the third largest pre-Christian population in the world; and,

WHEREAS we need to develop and implement strategies that view the U.S.A. as a mission field; and,

WHEREAS World Missions has been incredibly successful in its mission efforts and offers multiple methods by which the U.S.A. can be reached for Christ;

THEREFORE BE IT RESOLVED That we recognize the U.S.A. as a mission field; and,

BE IT FURTHER RESOLVED That the USA Missions ministry develop and deploy home missionaries and request missionaries from other ethnic and language groups from the international body who make up the Church of God; and,

BE IT FINALLY RESOLVED That we continue to develop means by which the ministries of World Missions and USA Missions work together in developing strategies and training workers for the world harvest.

III. CHURCH PLANTING DESIGNATED FUND (76th A., 2016, p. 184)

A designated church planting fund be established, with guidelines for securing and disbursing monies, to serve as a church planting "bank" from which matching funds and loans may be disbursed as funds are available to approved church planters who have met all established prerequisites. Furthermore, financial streams be developed to seed and grow the Church of God Church Planting Designated Fund with the goal of developing residual funding for perpetually assisting church planting. Further that this measure be inserted as an addition to the *Minutes - Church of God Book of Discipline, Church Order, And Governance,* where appropriate in order to secure the priority, establishment and longevity of the Church of God Church Planting Designated Fund.

S12. MINISTRY OF WORLD MISSIONS
(58th A., 1980, pp. 29-31; 68th A., 2000, pp. 78-80; 73rd A., 2010)

I. WORLD MISSIONS BOARD
A. Selection
The World Missions Board shall consist of not less than seven members who shall be appointed biennially by the International Executive Committee.

B. Duties and Authorities
This board shall concern itself with the worldwide ministries of the Church of God. Their duties and authorities shall be:

1. To develop and set forth the policy of the ministry of World Missions and its operation.

2. To consider and approve the annual budget of the ministry of World Missions for presentation to the International Executive Council.

3. To develop a worldwide strategy of evangelism, [and] education and conservation [of converts].

4. To interview, examine, and determine the eligibility of prospective missionaries.

5. To appoint all [World Missions] overseers, missionaries, educational coordinators, and presidents/directors of all educational institutions. Where practical, the tenure of national/territorial overseers of World Missions areas is for two years with a maximum tenure of twelve consecutive years in office (74th A., 2012).

6. To appoint all field directors and regional superintendents, subject to the approval of the International Executive Committee, and set their salaries.

7. To allow each country/territory flexibility in matters of polity to reflect cultural differences or government requirements, as long as the changes do not conflict with the doctrinal statements or Practical Commitments of the International General Assembly.

II. INTERNATIONAL COUNCIL
(66th A., 1996, Item 6, p. 62; 68th A., 2000, pp. 79, 80)

A. Purpose

To give greater involvement in order to support continued development of an international perspective in fulfilling the mission of the Church of God, and to ensure the sponsorship of ministries that meet the needs of persons of different cultural settings, the church must embrace a posture that includes both participation and representation in its general functions (Matthew 28:19; Mark 16:15; Acts 15:1-21). This posture should include specialized training programs and materials, opportunities for leadership experience, and open channels for new ideas. It should also provide a forum to discuss International General Council agenda items of concern to the international community and give opportunity for raising international issues for discussion.

B. Members

The International Council is composed of the following:

1. International Executive Committee
2. Director and assistant director of World Missions
3. Moderator of South Africa
4. Overseer of Indonesia
5. Two members (ordained bishops), at least one being African American and one Hispanic from the U.S.A., appointed by the International Executive Committee in consultation with the leadership of World Missions.
6. The field director and one selected representative (ordained bishop) from each of the following six areas (72nd A., 2008):

Africa	Canada	Europe
Asia-Pacific	Caribbean	Latin America

7. Others as approved by the International Executive Council (The manner of the selection of representatives is determined by each specific region which would be responsible for the travel expenses of its representative.)

C. Meetings
1. Meetings shall be moderated by the general overseer.

2. This council shall meet at least once every two years to provide input on an advisory basis to the International Executive Council on international issues and items of international interest for the agenda of the International General Council.

3. It shall meet prior to and with the International Executive Council (on related international issues) in the September of the off-Assembly years.

D. Function
The function of the International Council shall be to advise the International Executive Council on issues of international concern and to suggest possible items related to ministry in the international community for inclusion on the agenda of the International General Council.

III. DIRECTOR OF WORLD MISSIONS

A. Selection, Tenure, and Salary
The director of World Missions shall be nominated by the International General Council and elected by the International General Assembly quadrennially (4-year term, effective 2016). He shall be eligible to serve no more than four consecutive years. His salary shall be set by the International Executive Council (75th A., 2014).

B. Duties and Authorities
The director of World Missions shall:

1. Execute all the duties and assignments outlined by the World Missions Board.

2. Be the chief administrator of World Missions.

3. Recommend all prospective area superintendents.

4. Recommend all prospective personnel for approval by the World Missions Board.

5. Approve all convention dates in cooperation with the area superintendents.

6. Delegate any assignments necessary to the administrative assistants.

7. Be responsible for the preparation of the annual budget for the board's approval.

8. In conjunction with the chairman of the World Missions Board, disburse emergency funds as authorized by the board.

IV. Assistant Director of World Missions

A. Selection, Tenure, and Salary

The assistant director of World Missions shall be nominated by the International General Council and elected by the International General Assembly quadrennially (4-year term, effective 2016). He shall be eligible to serve no more than four consecutive years. His salary shall be set by the International Executive Council (75th A., 2014).

B. Duties and Authorities

The assistant director of World Missions shall:

1. Execute all the duties and assignments outlined by the director of World Missions and the World Missions Board.

2. Direct the program and assignments of the missions representatives. When area superintendents and missionary overseers are in the United States, he shall be responsible for assigning their deputational work as approved by the director of World Missions.

3. Be an official representative in world fields, state camp meetings, and conventions, as assigned by the director of World Missions [1982].

4. Recommend prospective missionaries to the director of World Missions.

V. Methods Used for Raising Missions Funds

1. State and regional overseers shall keep the cause of international missions before the ministers and laity, giving opportunity for special offerings in meetings in support of world missions (75th A., 2014).

2. The amount of tithes sent to the secretary general, and the percentage division of the amount sent, for the International Offices and World Missions, will be:

After September 1, 2014   5%   3.75%   International Offices
                                   1.25%   World Missions

3. Local church treasurers shall send the same amount as that for International Offices and World Missions (5%) in the amount sent

monthly, with their monthly report, to the state treasurer, from tithes paid into the local church. However, the division of the amount sent to the state treasurer shall be for the support of the state/regional office and home missions (72nd A., 2008; [2010]).

Note: For the amounts to be sent by the local church treasurer monthly, with their monthly report, from tithes paid into the local church, to the secretary general for International Offices and World Missions, and to the state treasurer for support of the state /regional office and home missions, see page 154 in this book.

4. Fifty percent (one-half) of all missions money raised in the district convention shall be kept in the state in which it was raised, to be used to evangelize new fields or, in case of emergency, used to assist small churches. The other 50 percent is to be sent to the secretary general for World Missions. All state overseers shall send their state convention missions offerings to the secretary general prior to the closing of the books for the fiscal year, except missions states, which shall be permitted to keep 50 percent of their district and state convention missions offerings for state missions work (40th A., 1945, p. 31; 56th A., 1976, p. 55).

5. Churches and individuals who so desire shall be granted the privilege of contributing directly to the support of any of our missionaries or international workers, and that such contributions may be sent to World Missions designated for the recipient of the gift (75th A., 2014).

6. Each state overseer shall remind the churches of their delinquency when they fail to raise their missions quotas regularly.

7. All prospective world missionaries shall be required to obtain a certificate of recommendation from the World Missions Board before they be allowed to solicit funds or supplies (37th A., 1942, p. 37).

VI. UNREACHED PEOPLE GROUPS (70th A., 2004, p. 54)

That our local churches be encouraged to adopt and intercede for an unreached people group. Resource materials will be provided by the ministry of World Missions.

Further, that all national churches of the Church of God international adopt and implement measurable steps to evangelize and disciple unreached people groups inside and outside of their own regions (Matthew 28:18-20; Romans 15:19-24; Revelation 5:9).

S13. PROCEDURE FOR FILLING VACANCY OF AN ELECTED MINISTRY LEADER

(67th A., 1998, p. 52; 73rd A., 2010)

A. Filling Vacancy of Ministry Leader

In the event the office of an elected ministry head becomes vacant because of death, disability, or the incumbent in any wise being disqualified, the assistant director of said ministry shall be elevated to the office of director.

B. Filling Vacancy of Assistant Ministry Leader

In the event the office of an elected assistant ministry head be vacated because of death, disability, advancement, or the incumbent in any wise being disqualified, the general overseer will submit by mail the names of the next two persons receiving the highest vote for that position, who were not elected to any general office, to the ordained bishops, to select the one who shall fill the vacancy in the ministry.

Ballots must be returned to the general overseer within 45 days to be valid votes. The one receiving the majority vote shall be declared to fill the unexpired term of the assistant to the ministry in question.

S14. MINISTRY OF CARE

(44th A., 1952, p. 34; 49th A., 1962, pp. 36, 37; 50th A., 1964, p. 52; [1972]; 55th A., 1974, pp. 55, 56; 73rd A., 2010)

I. BOARD OF DIRECTORS

A. Selection

Members of the Board of Directors of the Church of God Ministry of Care shall be appointed biennially by the International Executive Committee.

B. Duties and Authorities

The Ministry of Care Board of Directors shall:

1. Be responsible for all general institutions of benevolence, such as Home for Children, Home for the Aged, Home for Widows, and Home for Ministers.

2. Be responsible for all the disbursements of the Ministry of Care funds.

3. Adopt rules and regulations governing the admissions, the operation of the Homes, and to safeguard the interest of all persons who are admitted.

4. Approve all applicants recommended by the divisional leader for admissions to the Homes.

5. Provide for the general welfare of the persons in the Homes.

6. See that due care is used for the preservation of sanitary and healthful conditions in each Home.

7. Establish definite policies of sick leave for both professional and nonprofessional personnel.

8. Select, and set the salary of, the social services director of the Homes, subject to the approval of the International Executive Committee.

II. METHODS FOR RAISING HOME FOR CHILDREN FUNDS

Mother's Day shall be set apart as Home for Children Day, and a special offering shall be received for the Home for Children (49th A., 1962, p. 37).

III. HOME FOR CHILDREN—CANADA

The national moderator of Canada shall be authorized to establish and operate a Home for Children in Canada under the auspices of the general overseer and the national moderator of Canada (39th A., 1944, p. 29;[1972]).

S15. MINISTERIAL CARE, CENTER FOR
(59th A., 1982, page 42, item 4; [1996])

A Center for Ministerial Care shall be established by the International Executive Council, with accessibility at both general and state levels, including a toll-free telephone number.

The purpose of this center, staffed by experienced and qualified personnel, shall be to provide nurture and care for ministers and family members on a confidential basis and to restore troubled or erring ministers to emotional and spiritual health (Galatians 6:1, 2).

S16. CHAPLAINS COMMISSION (64th A., 1992, p. 84-86)

I. Name: Chaplains Commission
II. Chaplains Commission Board
A. Selection
The Chaplains Commission Board shall consist of not less than five members, who shall be appointed biennially by the International Executive Committee.

B. Duties and Authorities
The Chaplains Commission Board shall

1. Develop and set forth policies of the commission and its operation.

2. Consider and approve the annual budget of the commission for presentation to the International Executive Council.

3. Establish educational and pastoral standards for all commission endorsements.

4. Interview in person any applicant and spouse prior to final approval for military, institutional, hospital, prison, industrial, or campus chaplaincy, as well as for the specialized ministries of pastoral counselors, clinical pastoral education supervisors, and other pastoral specialists whose employment requires endorsement.

5. Annually review the work and denominational relationship of all endorsed personnel.

6. Delineate policies which enhance the commission's chaplaincy and specialized ministry programs.

7. Establish procedures in the supervision and discipline of endorsed personnel.

III. Chaplains Commission Director
A. Selection
The International General Assembly has created the office of director of Chaplains Commission. The International Executive Committee is authorized to fill the office.

B. Duties and Authorities
The Chaplains Commission director shall

1. Be responsible for the day-to-day operation of the commission.

2. Maintain a direct, functional, pastoral, and supervisory relationship with all endorsed personnel.

3. Screen and approve or disapprove all applications for volunteer and all part-time chaplaincy and specialized ministry personnel.

4. Submit an annual report to the International Executive Council of all commission activities.

5. Be the voting representative of the Church of God to national agencies and associations which foster understanding and promotion of chaplaincy and specialized ministry activities.

6. Be the Church of God liaison to all institutions allocating chaplaincy and specialized ministry positions.

7. Periodically visit all endorsed personnel as an expression of the church's support for these ministries.

Initially investigate and evaluate all questions or charges with regard to endorsed personnel's indiscretion and/or violation of church teachings, doctrines, or practical commitments and, if necessary, to submit written recommendations for further investigation and/or discipline to the designated state or territorial overseer.

S17. BOARDS AND COMMITTEES, GENERAL

I. STANDING BOARDS AND COMMITTEES (73rd A., 2010; see S7., II., 6)

1. We recommend that all standing [boards and] committees receive remuneration sufficient to cover their expenses when called together by the chairman or *ex officio* chairman (25th A., 1930, p. 21).

2. The chairman of each board shall be recognized as the proper authority to call all board meetings.

3. In the event the chairman should fail to do so, when necessity demands, any two members of the board shall have the authority to call a board meeting.

4. The general overseer, by virtue of his office, has the right to ask any board to meet, should he deem it necessary.

II. APPEAL BOARD

If an offending minister is not satisfied with the decision of a state board, he may appeal his case to the general overseer, who with his assistants and the secretary general may appoint a board to rehear the case, if in their judgment the case merits a new trial (33rd A., 1938, p. 50; 55th A., 1974, p. 53).

III. Emergency Board

The International Executive Committee is empowered to act as an emergency board.

IV. Trustees

A. Boards of Trustees

For the purpose of holding title to church properties (both real and personal) and the management of the same, there shall be a General Board of Trustees; State Boards of Trustees in the various states/territories, and countries; and Local Boards of Trustees in the various communities where local congregations exist. Any property (both real and personal) held by any of these boards is the property of the Church of God and shall be managed and controlled exclusively for the use and benefit of the Church of God (Cleveland, Tennessee, U.S.A.) (53rd A., 1970, pp. 43, 44; 62nd A., 1988, Journal, p. 49; [1994]).

B. General Board of Trustees, Members

The General Board of Trustees shall consist of seven members, two of whom shall be designated as alternates, appointed biennially at the International General Assembly by the International Executive Committee. Members of the General Board of Trustees so appointed shall hold office until their successors are appointed or until their positions on the board be declared vacant as hereinafter provided (53rd A., 1970, pp. 43, 44; 63rd A., 1990, p. 80).

C. General Board of Trustees, Duties and Authorities
(65th A., 1994, Item 11, p. 89; [1994]).

1. When the International General Assembly is not in session, any five members of the General Board of Trustees shall have power and authority to make all necessary transactions or arrangements for the sale or transfer of property, or for the borrowing of money and the pledging of real estate to secure the payment of the same, and to execute all necessary conveyances pursuant to the direction of the International Executive Committee (53rd A., 1970, pp. 43, 44; 62nd A., 1988, Journal, p. 49; 63rd A., 1990, p. 80).

2. WHEREAS, it is the policy of the Church of God (Cleveland, Tennessee, U.S.A.) that its general trustees hold title to all the real and personal property owned by, or held for the benefit of, the general church and its headquarters; but

3. WHEREAS, from time to time, certain individuals bestow property and other gifts upon integral agencies of the Church of

God (Cleveland, Tennessee, U.S.A.) and it is necessary that the board of directors of the integral agencies be authorized to receive said property or gift; now

4. THEREFORE be it resolved by the International General Assembly of the Church of God (Cleveland, Tennessee, U.S.A.) that these integral agencies of the Church of God (Cleveland, Tennessee, U.S.A.) are authorized and empowered to receive and hold title to real and personal property; with the duty, where legally possible, to recover to the general trustees of the Church of God (Cleveland, Tennessee, U.S.A.) under terms requiring such general trustees to hold title in accord with the conditions imposed by the device or gift (46th A., 1956, p. 30; [1994]).

Any person appointed to said General Board of Trustees shall be a member in good standing of the Church of God (Cleveland Tennessee, U.S.A.). If at any time, any member of any Board of Trustees shall cease to be a member in good standing, or if by reason of death, removal, incapacity, or unwillingness to perform all duties of his office, his place on the board may be declared vacant: on the general board by the general overseer, on a state board by the state overseer, on a local board by a local church conference; [and] the same power that declares said office vacant shall appoint a person to serve until the time for regular appointments, and the one so appointed shall have all authority held by the one removed (35th A., 1940, pp. 32-34; [1994]).

S18. EDUCATION, GENERAL BOARD
(52nd A., 1968, pp. 34-36; 53rd A., 1970, pp. 41, 42; [1972]; 65th A., 1994, Item 18, pp. 92, 93)

I. SELECTION (73rd A., 2010)

The General Board of Education shall consist of not less than five members (at least one of whom shall be from outside the United States), who shall be appointed biennially by the International Executive Committee.

II. DUTIES AND AUTHORITIES

1. To stimulate, nurture, and coordinate educational ministries in the Church of God.

2. To update and refine the Master Plan of Education at least every five years and to pursue its implementation.

3. To assist in the development, standardization, and evaluation of educational ministries at all levels in the Church of God.

4. To function in an advisory and consultative capacity to the educational institutions of the Church of God nationally and internationally without impinging upon the authority of the boards of control of these institutions.

To meet at least biennially (at the International General Assembly) in combined session with the presidents/directors and board chairmen of each institution of higher education and other educational leaders as appropriate.

III. INSTITUTIONS OF HIGHER EDUCATION

1. All Church of God agencies (national, state, and local) which desire to establish an institution of higher education should first secure permission from the International Executive Committee for research, study, and planning of such an institution.

2. Permission having been obtained, the agency should work with the General Board of Education in the projection of the plans for and details of operation of the new institution.

3. The results of the research, when finalized, shall be presented to the International Executive Council for approval, and permission to establish a Bible college or liberal arts college shall be granted by the International Executive Council.

S19. LEE UNIVERSITY

I. BOARD OF DIRECTORS

A. Selection

The Lee University Board of Directors shall consist of not less than seven members (two of whom shall be laymen), who shall be appointed biennially by the International Executive Committee (47th A., 1958, p. 33).

B. Duties and Authorities

The Lee University Board of Directors shall:

1. Be a legislative body and determine university policy.

2. Select and employ the university president, subject to the approval of the International Executive Committee.

3. Consider nominations of faculty and university personnel submitted by the president, with power to approve or veto. Upon failure of the president to nominate or renominate suitable persons for department heads, faculty members, or employees of the university, the board shall investigate reasons for his action, and if in their judgment such action is not warranted, any member of the

board shall have the privilege of nomination, which the board may approve or veto (46th A., 1956, pp. 22, 23).

4. In session with the president, set salaries of faculty members and other university employees. In session with the president, set prices for tuition, board, private lessons, and all other university fees. The board of directors shall have final jurisdiction of any and all charges brought against any faculty member. It shall approve an annual budget for operation of the university (41st A., 1946, p. 29).

5. Sign a contract and see that the president and all faculty members of Lee University sign a contract that they will not teach, publish, or allow to be taught or published, anything contrary to the Church of God Declaration of Faith or any other established doctrine of the church (43rd A., 1950, p. 16; 54th A., 1972, p. 55).

6. Permit no person unable or unwilling to accept in good faith the Church of God Declaration of Faith to be employed. In the event of the failure on the part of any faculty member to live up to said agreement the board of directors is authorized to dismiss him or her from the faculty.

II. Lee University President
A. Selection and Salary
The president shall be selected by the board of directors, who shall also set his salary.
B. Duties and Authorities
The board of directors shall define the duties and responsibilities of the president (53rd A., 1970, p. 39).

III. Vice President for Business and Finance
A. Selection
A suitable person shall be employed to fill the office of vice president for business and finance. He shall be selected in the same manner as other university personnel.
B. Duties and Authorities
The duties and responsibilities of the vice president for business and finance shall be determined by the board of directors (46th A., 1956, p. 23).

S20. MINISTRY OF PUBLICATIONS (73rd A., 2010)
I. MINISTRY OF PUBLICATIONS BOARD
A. Selection

The Ministry of Publications Board shall consist of seven members appointed biennially by the International Executive Committee (74th A., 2012).

B. Duties and Authorities

The Ministry of Publications Board shall:

1. With the general director of Publications, appoint, define the duties, and set the salary of all editorial and other personnel necessary for the operation of the publishing program of the church (52nd A., 1968, p. 36).

2. With the general director of Publications, have supervision of the Tennessee Music and Printing Company (46th A., 1956, p. 26).

3. Set up policies whereby the various ministries [of the Publishing House] may be coordinated (44th A., 1952, p. 32).

4. Give final decisions in all matters of business brought before it by the editors, the general director of Publications, or the employees (42nd A., 1948).

5. Pass upon the purchase of all machinery and other non-expendable material.

6. Set and maintain the editorial policies for all our publications (44th A., 1952, p. 32).

II. GENERAL DIRECTOR OF THE MINISTRY OF PUBLICATIONS
A. Selection and Salary

1. The general director of the Ministry of Publications shall be appointed by the International Executive Committee. He shall be executive head of the Ministry of Publications and shall be responsible for the total operations of the Publishing House.

2. The International Executive Council shall set his salary.

B. Duties and Authorities

1. The International Executive Council shall outline the areas of job responsibility of the general director of Publications.

2. He shall execute policies as set forth by the Ministry of Publications Board. He shall sign a contract that he will not teach,

publish, or allow to be taught or published, anything contrary to the Church of God Declaration of Faith, or any other established doctrine of the church. A copy of the Declaration of Faith shall be posted in the office of the general director of the Ministry of Publications.

III. EDITORIAL POLICIES

The editorial policies of Pathway Press shall reflect the doctrine, mission, vision, and core values of the church, and shall be determined by the General Publications Board in consultation with the International Executive Committee (75th A., 2014).

The name *Pathway Press* shall be adopted by the Publishing House to be used as an imprint on publications of such nature that they will have a potential market outside the Church of God [1974].

IV. CHURCH OF GOD EVANGEL (6th A., 1911, p. 10; 31st A., 1936, p. 35; [1972]; 55th A., 1974, pp. 54, 55; 73rd A., 2010)

The *Church of God Evangel*, being the official journal of the Church of God, is an effective means of acquainting our local congregations and ministers with the doctrine, polity, and various ministries of the Church of God, and is considered an official voice for Pentecost in the world today.

CHURCH GOVERNMENT—
MINISTRY
(S21 through S31)

S21. APPLICANTS FOR MINISTRY

I. MINISTERIAL INTERNSHIP PROGRAM (59th A., 1982, p. 43)

1. To more adequately ensure the formation of proper ministerial attitudes, and to offer a structured approach to practical ministerial training, each state or territory, where possible, shall provide beginning ministers with the opportunity to serve an internship under an experienced and competent pastor.

2. Guidelines for the internship program shall be established by the International Executive Committee and implemented by the Office of Ministerial Development in cooperation with overseers (57th A., 1978, pp. 36, 37).

II. INTERNSHIP REQUIREMENTS

In order to coordinate the present licensing requirements with the Ministerial Internship Program (MIP), the following measures are to be implemented:

1. Place questions concerning the ministerial candidate's involvement with MIP on the license application.

2. Coordinate the MIP reading list with required texts for various levels of ministry.

3. Require all MIP participants to be licensed at exhorter level, or be in the licensing process (having passed the examination and awaiting certification), before being eligible for the MIP program (70th A., 2004, p. 56).

4. Require all exhorters to participate in the MIP, or its equivalent, before being promoted to the rank of ordained minister. *Equivalent* shall be defined as the MIP reading requirement under the supervision of the state overseer, or one whom he appoints, plus one of the following:

- One year of pastoral ministry
- One year of evangelism ministry
- One year of associate pastoral ministry
- One year of specialized ministry listed on the ministerial report form (e.g. Chaplaincy, etc.) (75th A., 2014)

III. RULE REGARDING SETTING FORTH APPLICANTS FOR MINISTRY

The local church or churches should refrain from taking action on setting forth applicants for the ministry until the district overseer has conferred with the state overseer; and he [the district overseer]

BOOK OF DISCIPLINE, CHURCH ORDER, AND GOVERNANCE   97

shall be authorized to do so [approve setting forth the applicant] by the overseer of the state (25th A., 1930, p. 22).

IV. GENERAL REQUIREMENTS OF APPLICANTS FOR MINISTRY

1. All applicants for the ministry, including ordained bishops, ordained ministers, exhorters, ministers of music, and ministers of Christian education, must have the baptism in the Holy Ghost (21st A., 1926, p. 32; 50th A., 1964, p. 56; DF 8, 9).

2. All ministers shall adhere to the Teachings and Doctrines as set forth by the International General Assembly of the Church of God (75th A., 2014).

3. All ministers are required to pay tithes to retain their license (75th A., 2014).

4. All applicants for ministry shall serve as exhorters before making application for ordained minister certificate, except ordained ministers coming from other reputable organizations, licensed ministers of music, and ministers of Christian education (43rd A., 1950, p. 14 ; 50th A., 1964, p. 56).

5. All applicants for the ministry should be actively engaged in ministry before being recommended for credentialed ministry (75th A., 2014).

6. All applicants for the ministry, including those advancing in rank, must give consent to the state/regional office to conduct criminal background checks (70th A., 2004 p. 55).

7. International Exceptions. The following exceptions to the established ministerial credentialing process apply only to countries outside the United States and Canada:

   A. That the first two levels of credentials be issued by the field director's office, upon recommendation by the regional superintendent and national overseer, following appropriate screening and testing.

   B. That the history and polity sections of the examination for the first two ranks of ministry be redesigned to include an overview of the history and polity of the Church of God internationally, and a more detailed review of the national church history and polity where the examination is administered.

   C. The Ordained Bishop Examination will remain unchanged (77th A., 2018).

V. Divorced and Remarried Applicants (44th A., 1952, p. 35; 45th A., 1954, p. 29; 60th A., 1984, p. 43; 64th A., 1992, p. 81; 69th A., 2002, p. 49)

1. No applicant whose former spouse is living, or whose spouse's former spouse is living, shall be considered eligible for ministerial credentials except in cases where the divorce occurred because of the infidelity of the former spouse (see Matthew 19: 9); or that the divorce occurred prior to conversion (see 2 Corinthians 5:17) or due to abandonment by an unbelieving spouse (see 1 Corinthians 7:15). Conversion is interpreted as that point in time when one makes a public commitment to Christ, followed by a consistent Christian lifestyle. In no case shall this provision apply to one who once walked with Christ [lived as a Christian], but who later divorced and/or remarried while living in a backslidden condition.

2. The records of all such applicants shall be investigated and approved [or disapproved] by the respective state overseer, his council, and the International Executive Committee, prior to his or her being set forth [for the ministry] by the local church.

3. Applicants for ordained bishop who have a living former spouse, or whose spouse has a living former spouse, shall be approved by a two-thirds majority vote of the International Executive Council, before being set forth [for ordination] by the local church.

4. Persons with previous marriages, who now prove themselves faithful to God and to present family responsibilities, shall be permitted to hold the rank of exhorter, ordained minister, or ordained bishop, provided they are otherwise qualified.

5. Applicants for ministry who have more than one previous marriage ending in divorce, or whose spouse has more than one previous marriage ending in divorce, must be approved for any rank of ministerial credentialing by a two-thirds majority vote of their respective State/Regional Council, and by a two-thirds majority vote of the International Executive Council, before proceeding with the credentialing process, provided they are otherwise qualified (75th A., 2014).

VI. Honorary Certificates

That applicants for the ministry who have passed the age of retirement be granted honorary certificates, if they pass the state board examination and are endorsed by the general overseer. However, they will not be eligible for insurance, aged ministers' pension, or other financial benefits (44th A., 1952, p. 55; 50th A., 1964, p. 50).

BOOK OF DISCIPLINE, CHURCH ORDER, AND GOVERNANCE

VII. INTERNATIONAL MINISTERIAL CREDENTIALING (65th A., 1994, Item 13, p. 91)

All ministers duly ordained in the Church of God by a given national office may also receive an ordination credential from the International Offices of the Church of God, provided they apply through their respective area superintendents.

S22. ORDAINED BISHOP (68th A., 2000, pp. 80, 81; 71st A., 2006, p. 47)

I. THE MEANING AND USAGE OF THE TERM *BISHOP*

A. Biblical Understanding of Ordination

1. The offices of the church are ordained offices in a twofold sense.

First, the offices have been ordered or placed by the Lord as Head of the Church. The Scriptures name and define these offices by specific nomenclature and by description of functions. We may find it desirable to attempt to maintain Biblical nomenclature, but we must remember that the office is to find its primary meaning in the Biblical description of office and not in the title. The loss of Biblical title does not mean that Biblical function is abandoned or lost by loss of title or by shifting meanings of words in the contemporary setting.

Second, the persons placed in office are placed there by the calling of God and equipped by the Holy Spirit (1 Corinthians 12:1-11, 28, 29; Romans 12:4-8; Ephesians 4:11, 12). The equipment which the Lord provides incorporates both natural abilities and spiritual gifts.

2. Ministerial leadership offices include *bishops* (also called *elders* and *stewards*) and *deacons*. These leaders are not primarily operatives in an organization or hierarchy, but they are members of a living organism; therefore, the leaders and the led are members one of another. They partake of and transmit a common life drawn from a single life Source who is the Head of the body, Jesus Christ. This fact makes all the members of the body accountable to each other and each member responsible to promote the well-being of all others in the body. This also requires that every member have a relationship of submission to others in the body.

Leadership in the body of Christ is always related to the ministry of the Word, the grace of God, and the power of the Holy Spirit.

3. In addition to the ordination of the offices of the church, God also ordains individual members in particular offices/functions. Ordination must be understood as God's act. The church ordains

only in a secondary and responsive manner to the ordination that God has already established. As a responsive act, ordination by the church recognizes and honors God's ordination of persons in the body of Christ. This is also responsive to the individual minister who professes a particular calling or ministry. This is the corporate body's reverent "Amen" to the prior act of God, and to the professed calling of the minister.

4. The Church of God has chosen such terms as *Exhorter* (novitiate), *Ordained Minister* (intermediate level) and *Ordained Bishop* (the highest level of credentialed minister). These terms do not deal with the essential meaning of ordination; that is, they do not arise out of Biblical language and are not the products of Biblical exegesis. They are the products of a tradition in church polity, but they are not Biblical terms.

5. The act of ordination in the activity of the church is represented by such acts as the laying on of hands and sending ministers forth by the Holy Spirit in response to divine calling (Acts 13:1-4). Such an ordination seems also to be represented in the apostle Paul's statement of Timothy's designation for ministry by prophecy and the laying on of the hands of the presbytery (1 Timothy 4:14). The act of ordination, then, is the act of the church in affirming the call of God upon a minister, and sending the minister forth by the Holy Spirit.

6. It is appropriate for the church to require stages of the demonstration of calling and gifts. This evidence of calling and spiritual equipment should be observable in the life and ministry of the individual in the course of his/her fulfillment of ministry in the body of Christ. This demonstration of calling should be on a continuing basis in order to show the consistency of ministry and professed calling. No one should maintain credentials at any level of ministry who does not continue to show credible evidence of the Holy Spirit's calling and gifts in his/her service in the church.

7. It seems that the passage in Acts 13:1-4 is a paradigm of ordination. This ordination consists of the call of God, the approbation of the body of Christ represented in the laying on of hands, and sending the ministers forth under the power of the Holy Spirit.

Note the order and circumstances revealed in Acts 13:1-4. The body of believers described here included prophets and teachers. They were ministering to the Lord in fasting and praying. The Holy Spirit said, *"Separate unto me Barnabas and Saul for the work whereunto*

I have called them" (v. 2). The believers responded by continuing in fasting and praying. Finally, they *"laid hands on them and sent them away"* (v. 3). The climax of this narrative is, *"so, they being sent forth by the Holy Spirit, departed"* (v. 4).

Every act of sending forth is a responsive act on the part of the church to divine ordination. This order is also entirely consistent with that found in 1 Timothy 4:14.

8. That a study be done, and a theological paper prepared, defining the meaning and usage of the title Ordained Bishop; and should it be necessary, change the current nomenclature to clarify and fulfill the intent of the International General Council with respect to the designation of ministerial rank in the Church of God. Further, that this study be brought back to the 2016 International General Assembly, and that the results of this study be included in the **Minutes** of the International General Assembly of the Church of God (75th A., 2014).

B. New Testament Designation of Church Ministries and Offices

In the New Testament, there are three foundational texts that identify church ministries: Romans 12:4-8; 1 Corinthians 12:4-12, 28-30; Ephesians 4:11, 12. To these we may also add such texts as Acts 6:1-7 (for the ordination of the seven who relieved the Apostles by serving tables); 1 Timothy 3 (in the statement of qualifications for bishops and deacons); and Titus 1:4-9 (where the words for *bishop, elder,* and *steward* are used interchangeably).

From these sources we offer the following conclusions:

1. The terms *bishop (overseer), elder, steward,* and *pastor* are used in Scripture interchangeably.

This is not to say that these terms are synonymous, but they overlap in such ways that they are used to explain each other.

2. These offices by their application in Scripture are local in origin. Those who serve in these offices very often extend their ministries beyond the local level. In this way, they may serve many congregations (in modern terms, districts, states, regions, nations, geographic areas). When this is done, a local office becomes effective in broader areas of function.

3. In terms of the current polity of the Church of God, the following designations are recognized: *District Overseer, Administrative Bishop,* and *Presiding Bishop.* It is still the local definition that is basic to the meaning of the office. The only clear exception to this

conclusion is that of the *Apostles*, especially where that term is used of the Twelve and Paul.

4. It would not be consistent with the Biblical order of ministry to limit any one of these titles to a hierarchal group (such as district, state, nation or geographical area). This would imply that a local minister could no longer be called by his/her proper ministerial title. Therefore, pastors and others in spiritual oversight can be appropriately designated as *bishops*.

5. There is an implied hierarchy in a system that arranges Biblically equal titles according to territory or elevated placement in an organizational structure, but this is not Biblical order.

6. There are offices in Scripture (such as, *Apostles*) that have authority over other offices, but Scripture provides these precedents. These offices have their own titles and do not usurp and distort offices for which they have oversight. For example, the oversight authority of one office (such as, *administrative bishop*) in relationship to another office (such as, *pastor*) should not violate the legitimate authority of either office.

C. Use of the Title Bishop

We recognize that there may be cultural differences in various countries that would limit the usage of the title of *bishop*. In such cases, countries should be allowed to use the title as appropriate.

II. QUALIFICATIONS OF ORDAINED BISHOPS

1. The applicant for ordination as bishop must meet the Biblical requirements as set forth in 1 Timothy 3:1-7.

2. An applicant for ordination as bishop may be ordained when he is twenty-five (25) years of age, provided he has had at least eight (8) years of active ministry, or he has three (3) years of active ministry accompanied by a ministry-related degree or its equivalency from an accredited institution or one certified by the Church of God Division of Education, or when he is thirty (30) years of age, provided he has had at least five (5) years of active ministry, if he is otherwise qualified. In those cases in which a ministerial applicant has had verifiable active ministerial experience prior to receiving credentials, exceptions to the age qualifications can be made upon recommendation by the ministerial applicant's administrative bishop and with the approval of the Executive Council (72nd A., 2008; 76th A., 2016, pp.183-84).

3. In the case of military chaplains, the International Executive Committee shall be empowered to waive age, time, and performance minimums for ordination as bishop, if the applicant is otherwise qualified (51st A., 1966, p. 58).

4. Must have the baptism in the Holy Ghost (DF 8, 9).

5. Must successfully pass the examination given by a duly constituted board of examiners for ministerial candidates. It is understood that the examination will embrace areas of church government, doctrine, and general Biblical knowledge.

6. Applicants for ordination as bishop who have a living former spouse, or whose spouse has a living former spouse, shall be approved by a two-thirds majority vote of the International Executive Council before being set forth by the local church (64th A., 1992, p. 81).

7. The wife of the applicant for ordained bishop's license must be grave, not a slanderer, sober, and faithful in all things (41st A., 1946, p. 27).

8. It is understood that female ministers are not eligible for ordination as bishop (63rd A., 1990, p. 79).

9. Candidates striving to advance from the second rank of ministry to the third rank of ministerial credentials are encouraged, where feasible, to complete level two of the Certificate in Ministerial Studies or its approved equivalency.

III. RIGHTS AND AUTHORITIES (47th A., 1958, pp. 28, 29).

The ordained bishop shall have full right and authority to

1. Preach, publish, teach, and defend the gospel of Jesus Christ.

2. Serve as pastor and/or district overseer, or in other official capacities or appointments.

3. Baptize converts.

4. Receive believers into fellowship of church membership.

5. Administer Holy Sacraments (ordinances).

6. Solemnize rites of matrimony.

7. Assist in ordination ceremonies of fellow ministers.

8. Establish and organize churches.

9. Use the following titles while holding these specific positions:

State/Territorial Overseer (or international equivalency)
Administrative Bishop

International Executive Committee members
Executive Bishop

General Overseer
Presiding Bishop

10. In accordance with the agreement between the Full Gospel Church of God in South Africa and the Church of God, Cleveland, Tennessee, U.S.A., the ordained bishops of the Full Gospel Church of God in South Africa are members of the Church of God International General Council, and ordained bishops of the Church of God, Cleveland, Tennessee, U.S.A., are members of the General Council of the Full Gospel Church of God in South Africa, when visiting South Africa (46th A., 1956, p. 28; 68th A., 2000, p. 81).

S23. ORDAINED MINISTER (68th A., 2000, p. 81, 75th A., 2014)

I. QUALIFICATIONS OF ORDAINED MINISTERS

1. Must have the baptism in the Holy Ghost (DF 8, 9).

2. The candidate for ordained minister shall be actively engaged in ministerial activity.

3. Must adhere to the Teachings and Doctrines of the Church of God as set forth by the International General Assembly.

4. Must successfully pass the examination given by a duly constituted board of examiners for ministerial candidates. It is understood that the examination will embrace areas of church government, doctrine, and general Biblical knowledge.

II. RIGHTS AND AUTHORITIES (47th A., 1958, pp. 28, 29).

The ordained minister shall have full right and authority to
1. Preach, publish, teach, and defend the gospel of Jesus Christ.
2. Do the work of an evangelist.
3. Serve as pastor of a church.
4. Baptize converts.
5. Receive believers into fellowship of church membership.
6. Administer Holy Sacraments (ordinances).
7. Solemnize rites of matrimony.
8. Establish churches.

The ordained minister shall be privileged to sit in the International General Council without voting privileges.

An ordained minister may be ordained as bishop at the age of twenty-five (25) years, provided he has had at least eight (8) years in active ministry, or he has three (3) years of active ministy accompanied by a ministry-related degree or its equivalency from an accredited institution or one certified by the Church of God Division of Education, or at the age of thirty (30) years provided he has had five (5) years of experience in active ministry, if he is otherwise qualified. (76th A. 2016, pp. 183-184).

In the case of military chaplains, the International Executive Committee is empowered to waive age, time, and performance minimum for ordination as bishop (51st A., 1966, p. 72).

It is understood that female ministers are not eligible for ordination as bishop (63rd A., 1990, p. 79).

S24. EXHORTER
(20th A., 1925, p. 37; 45th A., 1954, p. 29; 65th A., 1994, Item 14, p. 91, (75th A., 2014; 77th A., 2018).

The church shall have an order of the ministry known as exhorter, whose license is signed by the district overseer where his membership is and endorsed by the state overseer.

I. QUALIFICATIONS OF EXHORTERS

1. The church recognizes the exhorter as a regular rank of the ministry. It is, however, the primary rank, and all applicants for the ministry must serve as exhorter before being promoted in rank, except ordained ministers coming from other reputable organizations.

2. Must have the baptism in the Holy Ghost (DF 8, 9).

3. The candidate for exhorter shall be actively engaged in ministerial activity before being recommended for licensing.

4. Must be thoroughly acquainted with, and adhere to, the Teachings and Doctrines of the Church of God as set forth by the International General Assembly.

5. Must successfully pass the examination given by a duly constituted board of examiners.

II. RIGHTS AND AUTHORITIES

The exhorter shall have full right and authority to

1. Preach and defend the gospel of Jesus Christ.

2. Serve as evangelist.

3. Serve as pastor of a church.

4. The exhorter may be authorized by the state overseer to baptize converts and receive believers into fellowship of church membership (47th A., 1958, pp. 28, 29; 77th A., 2018).

5. When an exhorter is serving as pastor, and where state laws recognize the credential of an exhorter as those of a duly authorized minister of the gospel, the exhorter may solemnize the rites of matrimony (54th A., 1972, p. 46).

6. The exhorter must be active in the ministry, and shall be required to pay tithes [into the local church where his or her membership is located] and to make monthly reports to the state overseer and to the secretary general. The exhorter may be promoted to the rank of ordained minister when deemed qualified by the state overseer and others concerned (42nd A., 1948, p. 27).

S25. FEMALE MINISTER (63rd A., 1990, p. 79; 68th A., 2000, pp. 81, 82)

Female ministers are to use the same ministerial titles as male ministers, with all the requirements, duties, responsibilities, and ministry opportunities of male ministers who hold either the first or second level of ministerial credentials as presently set forth in this book of *Minutes* of the International General Assembly. It is understood that female ministers are not eligible for ordination as bishop.

S26. MINISTER OF MUSIC AND MINISTER OF CHRISTIAN EDUCATION

I. QUALIFICATIONS OF MINISTERS OF MUSIC AND MINISTERS OF CHRISTIAN EDUCATION

1. Must have the baptism in the Holy Ghost (DF 8, 9).

2. Must be thoroughly acquainted with, and adhere to, the Teachings and Doctrines of the Church of God as set forth by the International General Assembly.

3. Must possess the necessary training, either formal or an adequate substitute thereof, to enable him [or her] to serve the church effectively in either of these highly specialized areas of the ministry.

4. Must successfully pass the examination given by a duly constituted board of examiners.

II. RIGHTS AND AUTHORITIES

The minister of music and/or minister of Christian education shall have full right and authority to

1. Serve as music director, Christian education director, teacher, or assistant pastor of local churches.

2. Publish, defend, and preach the gospel of Jesus Christ.

3. The minister of music and/or minister of Christian education shall not be eligible for ordination as long as he [or she] remains solely in the field of music or Christian education.

4. In the event the minister of Christian education or minister of music enters into a pulpit ministry, we recommend that he/she be given credit for his/her period of licensure [as minister of Christian education or minister of music] and that this period serve in lieu of the exhorter's licensure (50th A., 1964. p. 55).

S27. LAY MINISTER CERTIFICATION
(65th A., 1994, Item 12, pp. 89-91).

That a lay minister's certificate be issued to applicants who have a call of God into a specialized area of local church ministry where certification is deemed necessary and appropriate.

I. QUALIFICATIONS

The candidate must

1. Be a loyal member of the Church of God, adhering to its teachings.

2. Be baptized in the Holy Spirit.

3. Be faithful in tithing.

4. Be a regular church attendant.

5. Be one who works in harmony with the local, state, and international church's program and one who reflects a cooperative attitude toward the progress of the church.

6. Have completed at least one year of apprenticeship in local church ministry under the supervision of the pastor. The apprenticeship consists of successful completion of Mobilize: Local Leadership Development Program (levels 1 and 2), formerly called The Timothy Plan, now known as Mobilize.

7. Have the approval of the local church governing body with a recommendation from the pastor and church council.

II. RESPONSIBILITIES AND AUTHORITIES

1. The lay minister's certificate must be renewed every two years by the local church where the lay minister is a member.

Renewal requires that the individual continue to be actively engaged in one or more specialized areas of local church ministry, such as children's ministry, youth ministry, prison ministry, elderly ministry, music ministry, and so forth.

2. Whenever a lay minister transfers to another Church of God, the present certificate is terminated. The new church may approve the applicant and issue the lay minister's certificate. Once a person has completed the leadership development program and apprenticeship at one church, it is not necessary to repeat this process in order to be certified by another local church.

3. The lay minister shall serve as a helper to the pastor and shall be eligible to conduct various services and ministry activities sponsored by the local church under the supervision of the pastor.

4. The lay minister shall be authorized to represent the local church in the community as a certified Christian worker.

5. The lay minister shall teach and proclaim the gospel of Jesus Christ through areas of specialized ministry.

6. The lay minister shall serve as a model within the local church for the mentoring and discipling of believers.

7. Certificates are to be obtained from the state/territorial office.

S28. MINISTERIAL REPORTING

I. Forms for Monthly Reporting

In keeping with the financial system of the Church of God, it has been decided by the International General Assembly to furnish Report Forms upon request, in triplicate, to all ministers, for reporting to international and state headquarters on the first of each month.

II. Recording of Monthly Reports

The secretary general [his office] shall maintain the following record system for all ministers' reports.

1. Each report shall be recorded monthly on an individual record and summarized annually. A copy of said annual summary shall be placed in each minister's file and a duplicate copy mailed to the minister.

2. A permanent record shall also be maintained and filed in the vault [at International Offices].

3. All reports shall be electronically filed for permanent record before being destroyed.

III. Delinquent Reporting

1. When a minister becomes delinquent in reporting to international and state headquarters as much as three (3) months, he/she shall be urgently admonished by the state overseer of the state where he/she is ministering to bring his/her reports up to date.

2. Further, he/she shall be notified in writing that if he/she fails to report for a period of four (4) months, his/her license will be subject to revocation, after due disciplinary process (55th A., 1974, pp. 56, 57; 77th A., 2018).

S29. Instructions for Ministers
(68th A., 2000, p. 77; 71st A., 2006, pp. 47, 48)

I. General Instructions for Ministers

1. All ministers are expected to take care of their financial obligations promptly. Ministers who fail to maintain proper credit will be warned by the state overseer, and if satisfactory disposition is not made regarding financial obligations, the state overseer will refer the case to a state board for proper action (63rd A., 1990, p. 81).

2. All Church of God ministers should remain within the bounds of the decisions of the International General Assembly, and they are not to teach anything contrary to the Teachings authorized by this body (10th A., 1914, p. 31).

3. When a minister moves to another state without assignment, he/she is to notify his/her former and present state overseers at once. Further, he/she is to give his/her present state overseer information about himself/herself and family, previous ministerial work, what he/she would like to do, and how long he/she plans to remain in that state (45th A., 1954, p. 28).

4. Inasmuch as our ministers are expected to pledge full allegiance to the Church of God and its program, and inasmuch as we do not accept ministerial credentials from other organizations, licensing associations, or any other, we recommend that where our ministers hold such credentials they be required to surrender same; and where applicants to the ministry hold such credentials, they be required to surrender same before being approved for licensing (46th A., 1956, p. 25).

5. Believing a centralized form of government to be the Biblical (Acts 15:13-29) standard for our churches, the Church of God (Cleveland, Tennessee, U.S.A.) early adopted such a form of

government and has consistently practiced a centralized form of government [1994].

6. Be it therefore resolved that the International General Assembly does not recognize or approve the practice of our ministers setting up independent congregations who do not subscribe to the doctrines, faith, practices, teachings, and government of the Church of God.

7. Be it further resolved that we do not approve our ministers pastoring or otherwise assisting such independent congregations, and declare that ministers who persist in doing so are out of harmony with our stated policy of centralized government; and appropriate action should be initiated by proper authorities against offending ministers (46th A., 1958 p. 27).

8. No Church of God minister shall be required to violate a confidence, when such has been entrusted to him/her in the performance of his/her professional duties or in the course of his/her care of souls, except with the express permission of the person who has confided in him/her or in order to prevent a crime. This provision shall not preempt any applicable state or other required reporting laws, nor be used to conceal a felonious act toward another individual (51st A., 1966, p. 77; 74th A., 2012).

9. In order for any minister to be considered eligible for election or appointment by the International Executive Committee, General Council or General Assembly, the minister must be current on both personal ministerial reports and the local church reports with required finances from the church he/she pastors (if applicable). Any exceptions must be approved by the International Executive Committee. Further, this same measure applies to state/regional positions and boards. Any exception at the state/regional level must be approved by the state/regional overseer in writing (73rd A., 2010).

10. Responsible Use of Social Media: Christians are exhorted by Scripture to speak the truth in love (Ephesians 4:15), to provide things honest in the sight of all persons (Romans 12:17), and to do all things for the edification of others (Romans 15:2). The use of social media by believers should conform to these and other Biblical standards (74th A., 2012).

11. Any person placed/appointed/hired for a ministry position in a local congregation of the Church of God should have a criminal background check (77th A., 2018).

II. MARRIAGE AND SAME-SEX RELATIONSHIPS (75th A., 2014)

1. The Church of God rejects the cultural, political, and theological pressures to change the definition of marriage as being between one man and one woman. We affirm this definition based on God's Word and the truth that Christian marriage between a man and a woman reflects the theological truth of Christ's love for His Church.

2. Church of God ministers, whether an ordained minister or ordained bishop, shall only perform or participate in marriage ceremonies or marriage blessings between one man and one woman, as marriage is defined in the Bible. This policy also is applicable to Church of God ministers who serve in capacities outside the scope of normal pastoring, such as military, hospital, and corporate chaplains.

3. Local Church of God churches and the local Church of God ministers who serve them shall only hold, provide facilities for, conduct or preside over weddings, wedding receptions, and anniversaries (and other gatherings related to weddings, receptions, and anniversaries) that celebrate a marriage or blessing between one man and one woman, as marriage is defined in the Bible.

4. Church of God ministers shall maintain a Christlike attitude of love, mercy, and grace, when counseling or otherwise dealing with individuals in same-gender relationships. A Christlike spirit will maintain the truth of God's Word, the policies of the church, and avoid inappropriate remarks or attitudes that do not reflect the Holy Spirit.

5. Church of God ministers shall seek to find godly counselors to whom they can refer individuals in same-gender relationships for additional ministry and guidance.

6. Failure of Church of God ministers to adhere to these Biblically based guidelines will result in forfeiture of ministerial credentials.

S30. DISORDERLY MINISTERS [MINISTERIAL DISCIPLINE]

(68th A., 2000, pp. 72-77; 71st A., 2006, pp. 47, 48; [IE Council: January 2006])

INTRODUCTION: SCRIPTURAL PRINCIPLES

In Scripture the church is likened to a body of believers (1 Corinthians 12). It is to function in unity, diversity, and respect. It is to be sensitive to the needs of other members. When one suffers, all suffer; when one is honored, all are to rejoice (1 Corinthians 12:25, 26). The apostle Paul further instructs believers to rejoice with those who rejoice, and mourn with those who mourn (Romans 12:15). In this manner, members of the body of Christ affirm each other and minister to each other.

The discipline of a member of the body of Christ is a painful, but necessary experience. Since we are members of the same body, disciplinary action against any member, in reality, brings the whole body under judgment (1 Corinthians 12:12). Therefore all such action is to be undertaken in love and with a view toward restoration and reconciliation.

A minister who is found guilty of any of the violations of ministerial covenant and trust prescribed in these *Minutes* shall be disciplined for the purpose of restoration and maintaining accountability and integrity within the church and the ministerial body. The discipline and restoration process shall be based on Scriptural principles. It is in Biblical order, and it is consistent with the theology of grace and restoration, that a disciplined minister has an opportunity to be restored as a minister in the Church of God.

In Biblical usage, the concept of *restoration* carries the connotation of putting back together that which is broken, mending torn fishing nets, setting a broken limb, and restoring gently one who has fallen (Galatians 6:1). From the beginnings of humankind (Genesis 3:15), and throughout Biblical history (Revelation 3:19-22), the theme of the Bible is God's love for all people, even when they have disappointed themselves and turned from their relationship with Him.

I. FORGIVENESS AND RESTORATION

Forgiveness and restoration are distinct from each other in definition and purpose.

A. Forgiveness

1. *Definition:*

Forgiveness is the remission of sin by Christ in the extension of His grace and mercy. The role of the church is to be a community of the forgiven and the forgiving. Each member of the body, having been forgiven, is to be a forgiving member of the body. "And be ye kind one to another, tenderhearted, forgiving one another, even as God for Christ's sake hath forgiven you" (Ephesians 4:32).

2. *Purpose:*

The purpose of forgiveness is the renewal and continuation of fellowship in the body of Christ (Matthew 18:15-20). Forgiveness is not based on merit and is to be extended without counting (Matthew 18:21, 22).

B. Restoration
1. *Definition:*

Restoration is the "mending of the net" (Galatians 6:1), so that which is torn can be placed in service again. This spiritual mentality calls for all the members of the body of Christ to bear one another's burdens in the fulfillment of the law of Christ (Galatians 6:2-4).

Restoration is a conditional and rehabilitating process in which the offender demonstrates to the church and society that he/she is worthy of renewed trust and stewardship.

Renewal involves evidence of godly sorrow (2 Corinthians 7:9, 10), and a demonstration that the offender has cleared himself/ herself in the matters of offense (2 Corinthians 7:11).

2. *Purpose:*

The purpose of ministerial restoration is to place an offending minister back in a position of usefulness and activity appropriate to his/her demonstration of renewed spiritual capabilities.

The restoration process involves a team that is made up of the following: Ministerial Advocate, Administrative Bishop, a representative from the Center for Ministerial Care—in their respective country, mentoring pastor, and counselor (75th A., 2014).

C. Role of the Church

In both forgiveness and restoration the church is to confirm its love for the disciplined brother or sister and comfort him/her lest Satan gain an advantage (2 Corinthians 7:6-11).

II. DEFINITION OF TERMS

A. Suspension

As used in this section, the term *suspension* means the cessation of all ministerial activity, including ministerial voting privileges. During suspension, the minister may, under certain circumstances, maintain his/her membership in a group insurance program and/ or the Minister's Retirement Plan as provided by the policies of the Benefits Board. The cost of any personal insurance for which he/ she may be eligible during the period of suspension shall be the responsibility of the minister.

B. **Revocation**

As used in this section, the term *revocation* means the termination of ministerial credentials with the Church of God, including all the rights and privileges appertaining thereto.

III. DISORDERLY CONDUCT

A. **Explicit Heterosexual Misconduct**

1. Any minister found guilty of adultery, fornication, or other sexually explicit heterosexual misconduct shall have his/her ministerial credentials suspended/revoked for a minimum period of two years. Should said minister desire reinstatement of credentials, he/she shall submit to the prescribed program of restoration through the office of the Center for Ministerial Care (75th A., 2014).

2. At the discretion of the state/territorial overseer and state/territorial council, the minister may be allowed to engage in limited, supervised ministerial activity during the second year of the disciplinary period.

3. At the conclusion of the two-year period, upon successful completion of the restoration program, and with the recommendation of the state/territorial overseer, the International Executive Council shall make a decision concerning the reinstatement of credentials and at what level. (See **S5. International Executive Council, III. Duties and Authorities,** Item 11.)

4. Any minister found guilty of sexual abuse of a child or a second offense involving adultery, fornication, or any other sexual misconduct, or any combination of these offenses, shall have his/her credentials permanently revoked. He/she must be disfellowshipped from the church. However, the opportunity for reconciliation and restoration to church membership shall be given future consideration in appropriate cases (72nd A., 2008).

B. **Other Heterosexual Misconduct**

1. Any minister found guilty of any other heterosexual misconduct shall have his/her ministerial credentials suspended for a minimum period of one year. Should said minister desire reinstatement of credentials, he/she shall submit to the prescribed program of restoration.

2. At the discretion of the state/territorial overseer and state/territorial council, the minister may be allowed to engage in limited,

supervised ministerial activity after the first six months of the disciplinary period.

At the conclusion of the one-year period, upon successful completion of the restoration program, and with the recommendation of the state/territorial overseer and the approval of the International Executive Council, the minister shall be reinstated to his/her former rank of ministry. (See **S5. International Executive Council, III. Duties and Authorities,** Item 11.)

C. **Unbecoming Conduct**

1. Any minister found guilty of unbecoming ministerial conduct shall be disciplined under a plan determined by the state/territorial overseer, in consultation with the trial board. Disciplinary options shall include official reprimand, restitution, censure, remedial action, reexamination, restrictions, and, where necessary, suspension of credentials.

2. Unbecoming ministerial conduct shall be defined as violations of personal integrity, of doctrinal fidelity as accepted by the Church of God, and of leadership accountability.

3. For any violation of doctrinal fidelity, re-examination at the appropriate level shall be required.

4. For any suspension of credentials under this section, the offending minister shall submit to the prescribed program of restoration for a minimum period of one year.

5. At the discretion of the state/territorial overseer and state/territorial council, the minister may be allowed to engage in limited supervised ministerial activity during the last six months of his/her suspension. At the conclusion of the disciplinary period, upon successful completion of the restoration program, and with the recommendation of the state/territorial overseer and state/territorial council and the approval of the International Executive Council, the minister shall be reinstated to his/her former rank of ministry.

6. Any minister found guilty of more than one violation of unbecoming ministerial conduct shall have his/her entire disciplinary record submitted to the International Executive Council for a determination as to continued ministry or permanent revocation of credentials (68th A., 2000, pp 76, 77).

D. **Homosexual Offense**

The credentials of a minister must be revoked when found guilty of a homosexual offense, and he/she must be disfellowshipped from the church. He/she is never to be reinstated to the ministry (43rd A., 1950, pp. 18, 19; 46th A., 1958, p. 27; 50th A., 1964, p. 54).

IV. PROGRAM OF RESTORATION

Any minister whose credentials have been suspended/revoked shall be offered a program of restoration. The restoration process shall be facilitated by the Center for Ministerial Care office and involve ministry from the entire church body (75th A., 2014).

A. Supervision

In the Church of God, the prescribed program of restoration is supervised by the International Executive Council and implemented by a ministry team including, but not limited to the following: the ministerial advocate, the state/territorial overseer, the local church, a pastoral mentor, a Christian counselor, and the Center for Ministerial Care.

B. Coordination

The Center for Ministerial Care shall coordinate the ministry team and serve in a facilitative and consultative role. (Any exceptions to this procedural approach, such as in areas outside the United States of America, shall be approved by the office of the ministerial advocate.)

C. Procedures

1. The disciplinary process officially begins when the minister enters the restoration program by notifying the Center for Ministerial Care in writing on the forms provided.

2. If requested, the person being disciplined shall be allowed up to three months to make necessary emotional, vocational, and family adjustments prior to entering the restoration program, provided the limits on ministerial activities are observed.

3. Should a minister whose license has been suspended, fail to voluntarily enter the restoration program within three months from the date of being advised by the state/territorial overseer of the disciplinary action and the requirement to enter the restoration program, said minister's credentials shall be revoked.

D. Healing and Renewal

The disciplined party must show evidence of healing and renewal of strength against the temptations that provoked his/her failure. This is to be demonstrated by:

Confession of the shame and ramifications of his/her offense.

Acceptance of personal blame and responsibility for the offense.

Submission to the authority of the church in its disciplinary and restorative processes.

E. Whereas the Church of God believes in the restoration of the individual; and whereas the Church of God makes such provision for the restoration of credentialed ministers who successfully complete care counseling; and whereas there is a wealth of potential ministers among the Church of God laity; be it resolved that any lay member with past disqualifying behaviors, who successfully completes a restorative care program (Church of God), and is otherwise qualified for credentialed ministry, be considered for possible licensing (75th A., 2014).

V. Additional Rulings—Disorderly Ministers

1. The disciplinary record of all ministers shall be cumulative and the entire record shall be considered in all disciplinary actions.

2. In the event the individual being disciplined is not credentialed by the Church of God, but is engaged in ministerial activities, the policies relating to suspension and revocation of ministry as defined in this section shall apply (68th A., 2000, p. 77).

3. All ministers having their ministry revoked for the cause of failure to pay tithes shall be required to show a record of at least six (6) months of loyalty in tithing before being reinstated to the ministry (33rd A., 1938, p. 49; 56th A., 1976, p. 55).

4. Ministers who resign their ministry to evade charges instituted, or being instituted against them as a result of alleged offending conduct, shall be considered guilty (46th A., 1956, p. 23).

5. Where ministers have had their ministry revoked for any cause and engage in ministerial activities in opposition to the Church of God, our ministers and members shall be considered disloyal in promoting their ministerial activities (44th A., 1952, p. 31).

6. Where a minister's work has been generally known, either before or after he/she surrendered his/her license, his/her application for reinstatement to the ministry shall be approved by a two-thirds vote of the International Executive Council, and the general overseer shall determine whether or not his/her case should come before the International Executive Council (43rd A., 1950, p. 16).

7. A minister whose license is revoked and who goes into open sin shall be required to be baptized in water before his/her ministry is restored, and we further recommend that this apply to any and all ministers who shall apply for membership in the Church of God (37th A., 1942, p. 36).

8. The past record of ministers who present themselves to the Church of God shall be investigated; and where there have been accusations of immoral conduct, said ministers shall not be eligible to be an ordained minister or an ordained bishop until endorsed by three-fourths of the International Executive Council (36th A., 1941, p. 47).

9. When a minister has been tried by a state board and his/her license ordered revoked, and the local church where his/her membership is instructed to withdraw fellowship, the local church shall be required to carry out the decision of the state board. Further, where the offending minister has been found guilty of the sexual abuse of a child, an offense that requires withdrawal of church membership and permanent revocation of ministerial credentials, the guilty party shall be prohibited from attending, participating in, or having any involvement with, any activities of the local church or churches where the victims in said offense presently attend or have attended (36th A., 1941, p. 48; 74th A., 2012).

10. Ministers who do not report or who are not actively engaged in preaching and other ministerial work for as much as six (6) months, provided such inactivity is not caused by illness or age, shall have their ministry revoked (35th A., 1940, p. 35).

11. The minister who allegedly walks disorderly while in another state, should be tried by a state board in the state where the alleged offense was committed, and if found guilty his/her ministry should be revoked by the overseer of the state where his/her membership is (23rd A., 1928, p. 41).

S31. OFFENDING MINISTERS
I. MINISTERIAL DISCIPLINE (63rd A., 1990, pp. 70-75)
Trial Procedures and Appeals for Church of God Ministers

Inasmuch as Church of God hearings and/or trials of its ministers or members are ecclesiastical rather than civil in nature, and concern matters within the Christian brotherhood, to be judged by the guidelines of Holy Scripture rather than civil law, the ministers and members of the Church of God do hereby agree that legal counsel may not attend or participate in those proceedings.

However, the accused, as well as the person bringing the charge shall be given the option of inviting a duly credentialed Church of God minister to appear with him/her throughout the hearings, trials, or appeals for the purpose of personal support only. Further, in matters of alleged sexual, physical, or psychological abuse by the accused, where there may be alleged victims or witnesses to the same, each of those alleged victims or witnesses shall be given the option of inviting a duly credentialed Church of God minister to appear with him/her throughout hearings, trials, or appeals for the purpose of personal support only (74th A., 2012).

A. Guidelines for State Overseers

1. Warn ministers who are delinquent in reporting.

2. Revoke the license of ministers who have not reported for as much as six (6) months.

3. Arrange for trial of accused ministers, notifying the accused of charges, time, and place of trial.

4. Terminate the license of a convicted minister by signing a revocation which is sent to the general overseer.

5. Revoke the ministry of one who is a member of his state when his/her trial, conviction, and offense were in another state.

6. In rare instances involving church and pastor estrangement, a board of three (3) ministers appointed by the state overseer might be of some help to the overseer. Such a board could listen to problems and render an advisory opinion. This type of procedure, in acute cases, furnishes a broader base of strength for the overseer.

7. In instances of increasing rumor and/or question, the state overseer could appoint a board of investigation to separate fact from rumor, provide a clearer conception of the problem at hand, and possibly indicate a proper course of action.

B. Trial Procedures

1. Filing of Charges

Any charge brought against a minister must be in writing and signed by the individual bringing the said charge. Prior to any formal trial or hearing, the state overseer shall, where possible, arrange a face-to-face meeting between the accused and the accuser, in keeping with the commands of Jesus in Matthew 18:15-17. Said meeting to be moderated by the state overseer, or one whom he shall appoint.

    a.   The burden of proof rests upon the individual making the charge.

b. Refuting said charge rests upon the one charged.
c. Any charge should be presented to the state overseer of the state in which the alleged offense is committed.
d. After a charge is brought in writing, the burden of handling said charge rests with the state overseer, who is considered the pastor of any minister serving under his charge.

2. **Selection of Trial Board**
The state overseer shall appoint all trial boards.
   a. He should avoid using the State Council as a trial board. However, individual members of any elected board can be selected by the administrative bishop, if he chooses (75th A., 2014).
   b. All members of a trial board should be individuals of experience, such as a pastor or evangelist.
   c. The trial board should consist of not less than three (3) ordained bishops.
   d. Conflicts of interest, such as relatives, those taking sides, or those connected in any way which would hinder a fair trial or cast a shadow upon the system of the church to deal ethically or fairly with all men should be avoided.
   e. Any minister appointed to a trial board who feels he cannot render an impartial decision should so state and be replaced.
   f. Any officer in the trial procedure who feels there is a conflict of interest should have the right to call said conflict to the attention of the state overseer or the general overseer and expect it to be corrected before proceeding with consummation of the trial.
   g. Any ministerial liaison or advocate who is subjectively involved, or whose family is involved, should have the right not to participate in any decisions related to the case, absent himself voluntarily, and request to be replaced for any given trial.
   h. The accused minister, as well as the person making the accusation, shall be given the option of inviting another duly credentialed Church of God minister to appear with him/her during hearings, trials, and appeals, for the purpose of personal support. (Since this is an ecclesiastical matter in the

brotherhood of the church, no legal counsel may be present) (75th A., 2014).

3. Notification of Defendant

The state overseer shall set the date of trial and notify defendant of charges, time and place of trial, at least seven (7) days prior to trial. Notification shall be given by certified mail with a return receipt, where possible. If defendant waives the time limit in favor of an earlier trial, he/she should sign a statement to that effect which will become a part of the trial record. The defendant may, with the consent of the state overseer, waive trial by the state board to a board appointed by the general overseer and his assistants, in which case there shall be no appeal.

4. Consideration for Person Making Charge

    a.   The right of fair and courteous treatment
    b.   The right to be instructed concerning all procedures
    c.   The right to produce witnesses with corroborating testimony and evidence
    d.   The right of notification of trial, procedures, and the right of appeal
    e.   The right to appeal any conflict of interest which might occur
    f.   The right to be heard, to face the one being charged, and to face those hearing said charge

5. Consideration for Person Charged

    a.   The right to be considered innocent until proven guilty, in accordance with our trial system
    b.   The right to know what he/she is charged with and the person(s) bringing the charge (in writing)
    c.   The right of fair and courteous treatment
    d.   The right to be instructed concerning all procedures
    e.   The right to plead "guilty" or "not guilty"
    f.   The right to refute said charges and to produce witnesses, testimony, and other evidence
    g.   The right to be heard, to face the accuser and those hearing said charges, and to be present in the hearing room while evidence is being heard

h. The right of appeal concerning any conflict of interest which might occur
i. No defendant can avoid a trial by board by confessing to a lesser charge. Trial by board can be avoided only by confessing to the greater charge. For example: any confession of "unbecoming conduct with the opposite sex" must be tried by board to determine that indeed the individual is not guilty of the greater charge of "adultery."

6. Trial Procedures

a. Secretary of Record—the state overseer shall appoint a secretary to keep a record of trial proceedings.
b. Register of Witnesses—both the defense and prosecution shall furnish a list of witnesses prior to the trial. Testimony should then be limited to these witnesses, unless one comes forward during the trial with new evidence.
c. The Trial—the state overseer shall moderate the trial unless the defendant is related to him, in which case he shall disqualify himself and the moderator shall be appointed by the general overseer. The trial should be opened with prayer, followed by appropriate remarks by the chairman. The charges should be read to the defendant in the presence of the person(s) who signed the charges. The charges shall then become a part of the trial record.
d. When a group of individuals has preferred charges, they may testify individually or they may select a spokesman from their number to represent them, provided the defendant is so notified and offers no objection. However, in morals cases each witness must testify individually. In all cases, individual testimony must be given if the defendant so desires.
e. After all prosecution witnesses have testified, the defendant shall be given an opportunity to face each witness individually and to defend himself/herself. After the defendant has had opportunity to face his/her accusers, defense witnesses will then be called and heard individually. Character witnesses may be heard individually or collectively at the discretion of the board.

f. The board shall retain the prerogative to recall any witness on either side at any time during the trial. The board may go into executive session at any time in order to clarify testimony, discuss possible changes in procedure, or determine what action present circumstances may dictate.

7. *Notification of Decision*
   a. When all testimony has concluded, the defendant shall be excused and told that he/she will be notified of the board's decision. In most instances, the defendant can be notified in person or by telephone, and the decision confirmed by certified mail, where possible. After deliberation, the board shall present its decision in writing, signed by each member, to the state overseer, who in turn will notify the defendant and the complainant and take appropriate action.
   b. The trial board's decision will become part of the defendant's permanent record at the state office and will also be filed at International Offices (74th A., 2012).
   c. In the event the trial board renders a decision of guilt, said decision must be in agreement with the ruling of the International General Assembly listed under caption **S30. DISORDERLY MINISTERS.**
   d. Both the one charging and the one being charged should be notified of the decision of the trial board, and (a) recommendations for conforming to said decision and/or (b) a record of this follow-up should be kept in the individual's file.

II. Appeals

A. Any appeal from a decision of a state trial board must be presented to the general overseer in writing and signed within ten (10) days after the defendant has received written notification of the decision from the state overseer.

B. An appeal may be granted when requested in writing within the prescribed time limit for one or more of the following reasons:
1. The trial was conducted improperly.
2. New evidence which was not available at the time of the trial becomes available.
3. There is a conflict of interest in those conducting the trial.

4. The International Executive Committee deems such advisable for other reasons.

Note: Every minister has a right to expect courteous treatment and fair dealing from his/her superiors in all matters relating to his/her position or field of labor in keeping with the dignity of a minister of the gospel. In the event these rights are apparently denied, and by this denial his/her ministry shall be greatly curtailed and damaged, he/she shall have the right to appeal to the general overseer, in writing, who, with the International Executive Committee, shall take whatever steps are necessary to effect a possible solution, if in their opinion the appeal warrants such action. The purpose of the right of appeal is to open channels whereby differences between the concerned parties may be resolved (54th A., 1972, pp. 54, 55).

CHURCH GOVERNMENT—STATE
(S32 through S45)

S32. STATE OVERSEERS (Administrative Bishops, see p. 103.)
(60th A., 1984, pp. 42, 43; 73rd A., 2010, 75th A., 2014)

I. SELECTION
1. State overseers shall be appointed by the International Executive Committee, and a rating instrument shall be designed to indicate the state overseers' performance, and this rating sheet shall substitute for the preference ballot as the primary source of information. Also, that a place be provided on the rating sheet for the individual's preference for state overseer. Only performance sheets with state overseer preferences that are returned will be counted in the reappointment of state overseers.

2. That the opportunity to participate in the State Administrative Bishop Preference/Evaluation voting process be restricted to those credentialed ministers who are current with their personal ministerial reports to both their State/Regional Office and the International Offices. In addition, those ministers who have been appointed as a pastor of a local church must also be current, or in covenant agreement, with their state/region and international monthly church reports, including appropriate monies, beginning at the time of their appointment, in order to participate in the process.

3. Further, that all credentialed ministers be active in both tithing and attendance in a local Church of God congregation within the state/region in which the vote/evaluation is conducted (77th A., 2018).

II. QUALIFICATIONS
The office of state overseer is an honored and vital position in the Church of God (Acts 20:28). It is therefore fitting that the person who serves in this capacity be a person of strong spiritual authority and able to demonstrate capable leadership qualities, such as

1. The ability to oversee persons as well as programs (Acts 20:28).

2. An attitude of submission to those over him in the Lord (Hebrews 13:7).

3. Leadership qualities to motivate and delegate responsibilities for efficient operation (1 Corinthians 16:1; 1 Timothy 1:18, 19; 5:1, 2).

4. Sensitivity to those whom he serves by exemplifying compassion, trustworthiness, concern, and integrity (Hebrews 6:10; 1 Timothy 1:18, 19; 4:12, 13; 6:12; 1 Thessalonians 2:1-12; 2 Corinthians 4:1-3; 6:3-12a).

5. Adaptability to the cultural differences and changing role of church ministry (Acts 6:1-7; 2 Timothy 4:1, 2).

6. The state overseer shall have served as the senior/lead pastor of a local church congregation for a minimum of five (5) years, or after having been elected to an International Office or Position in the Church of God. (Anyone under appointment as an Administrative Bishop, or as a Youth and Discipleship director, as of the 2018 General Assembly, shall be exempt from this requirement) (77th A., 2018).

III. Accountability

1. He shall be accountable to those who appoint him and dedicated to those whom he serves (2 Timothy 2:4, 5; Luke 16:2).

2. He shall be a model by demonstrating Christlike attributes in his lifestyle and administration (2 Corinthians 6:3, 4a).

3. He shall be diligent in his relationship with his family, his community, his colleagues, and those over him in the Lord, so as not to bring a reproach to his witness and position (1 Timothy 3:2, 4, 5; 1 Corinthians 12:18, 20, 25, 28-30; 1 Thessalonians 5:12, 13; Romans 14:16; James 4:11; 1 Timothy 6:12, 14; 2 Timothy 2:24, 25).

4. He shall stay abreast of the times in terms of administration, finances, office procedures and techniques, and communications.

5. He shall be evaluated periodically by the International Executive Committee.

IV. Orientation

Overseers who are appointed for the first time shall be given a period of orientation immediately following their appointment by the International Executive Committee.

V. Term of Office (64th A., 1992, p. 88; 69th A., 2002, p. 48, 75th A., 2014)

The state overseer's term of office shall be for four years (beginning with the 2016 International General Assembly term). Any additional terms must meet the following criteria:

1. He must receive a minimum of a two-thirds majority of the vote of the ministers [in his state or region].

2. The success of his administration must merit said consideration for an additional term.

3. The International Executive Committee must believe his reappointment to be in the best interest of the state.

The tenure of office [for the state overseer] is for a maximum of 12 years in non-mission states. He may serve all or part of his tenure in any state or number of states depending upon the above-stated criteria. He may be eligible for reappointment as a state overseer after serving in some other capacity for at least two years.

VI. CONTINUING LEADERSHIP DEVELOPMENT

State overseers shall actively participate in continuing leadership development and training courses as planned, directed, and implemented by the International Executive Committee (77th A., 2018).

VII. DUTIES AND AUTHORITIES (25th A., 1930, p. 21; 28th A., 1933, p. 43; 39th A., 1944, p. 23; 41st A., 1946, p. 26; 42nd A., 1948, pp. 28-30; 44th A., 1952, p. 35)

The state overseer shall:

1. Arrange for and assist in conducting a general evangelistic campaign throughout his state or territory.

2. Appoint district overseers, pastors, and make changes or fill vacancies in pastorates, when necessary.

3. Approve the setting in order of churches before organization is effective.

4. Approve the selection, purchase, and construction of all church, parsonage, or Sunday school properties, together with the respective district overseers.

5. Officiate at all ordination services in his territory, sign credentials of all ministers in his territory who have been approved by the general overseer, or return such credentials to the general overseer, giving reasons for not signing.

6. Sign revocation when terminating the ministry of any individual.

7. Discontinue inactive churches; sign a report of same on forms prepared for this use and send to the general overseer.

8. Transfer members of churches which have ceased to exist, to the church most convenient for the member.

9. Appoint any officer in a local church, Family Training Hour and/or YPE, Sunday school, or Women's [Discipleship] Ministries, when necessary.

10. Pass on all questionnaires of applicants to the ministry in his territory who are considered worthy, and sign such applications, showing his endorsement of the applicant before submitting applications to the general overseer.

11. Decide the bounds of each district in his state or territory.

12. Report the organization of new churches to the secretary general on forms prepared for same.

13. Conduct a convention on each district once each year, or group two or more districts for one convention, and at least one state convention, giving general instructions in doctrine and general interests of the church.

14. Call district or state ministers' meetings or prayer conferences to arrange for the state program.

15. Before launching large financial state projects, have the approval of the International Executive Committee.

16. Where the state overseer is serving as pastor, or has relatives who are members of the church, or other conditions that would render him incapable of giving a fair trial to an offending member who has been excluded from the church, he has a right to appeal to the general overseer, who shall select two ordained bishops to sit with him to decide whether or not the offending party should have another trial.

17. The state overseer, with the district overseer, may authorize exhorters to pastor churches, baptize, and receive members into the church, when such authority is necessary or in case of an emergency.

18. The state overseer shall make monthly reports to the general overseer on forms prepared for such reports.

19. Leave all records pertaining to the state work, such as minister's reports, church treasurer's reports, ledgers, financial records, state board decisions, or any other record of importance, in the files in the state office for his successor's information.

20. Live in the state or province over which he is made overseer.

21. To model, encourage and provide formal training and prayerful guidance to pastors in the following areas: Preparing and managing an annual local church budget; dealing with local church conflict resolution; and impacting the local community (74th A., 2012).

22. That each state/regional office conduct an annual Ministry Life Planning Training event covering the issues and challenges of retirement planning, ministerial retirement transition, ministerial taxes, healthcare, and whole life health, to assist ministers of every age to approach the stages of life successfully, and to embrace the aging of ministry (77th A., 2018).

23. That each state/regional overseer, in cooperation with the state/regional Youth and Discipleship director, lead pastors, student pastors, and the state/regional Ministerial Development Board (CAMS and MIP), adopt an annual plan for identifying, mentoring/training, and engaging young men and women, designated as the "Jeremiah Generation," in both the local and state/regional ministry of the Church of God (77th A., 2018).

S33. STATE COUNCIL

I. SELECTION

The ministers of each state, in conference, shall elect a board of councilors to the state overseer (the state overseer serving as *ex officio* chairman) after the following manner:

1. States having 251 or more churches elect not less than 12 ministers.

2. States having 91-250 churches elect not less than 10 ministers.

3. States having 61-90 churches elect not less than eight ministers.

4. States having 21-60 churches elect not less than six ministers.

5. States having up to 20 churches elect not less than four ministers (63rd A., 1990, pp. 79, 80).

With the exception of national, territorial, provincial, or mission states, all councilmen must be ordained bishops. When sufficient ordained bishops are not available in national, territorial, provincial, or mission states, ordained ministers may be appointed as councilmen by the general overseer and respective state overseer (51st A., 1966, p. 62).

II. DUTIES AND AUTHORITIES

The State Council shall:

1. With the state overseer, have supervision of the state missions money, surplus tithes, state parsonage, campground, and all other funds received and disbursed by the state treasury.

The proceeds from the sale of property of disbanded churches, less expenses incurred by the state/regional offices for that particular church, shall be disbursed exclusively for church assistance and church planting (73rd A., 2010).

2. After state office expenses have been paid, be authorized to use the surplus tithe of tithes from the state treasury to supplement

the income of underpaid pastors and evangelists (43rd A., 1950, p. 15; 45th A., 1954, pp. 29, 30; [1974]).

3. Meet as often as the ministers and the overseer [in the state] deem necessary.

4. Consider and pass on appeals and applications for help on new projects, evangelism, needy ministers, or such emergencies as may arise from time to time.

5. Counsel and act with the state overseer in the study and preparation of recommendations for the State Ministers' Conference (43rd A., 1950, pp. 19, 20).

6. With the state overseer, employ the state secretary and treasurer and set salary, and so forth. However, where the state overseer receives the limit in salary and expense, no member of his immediate family shall be employed as state secretary and treasurer.

S34. STATE BOARD OF TRUSTEES

1. In each state, territory, or country where needed, the state overseer shall, at a state meeting or called meeting of the ministers of the church, or at a state convention of the membership of the church, appoint a State Board of Trustees of not less than five members. (Any three members of the said board, with the consent of the state overseer, shall have authority to make all necessary transactions or arrangements for the sale or transfer of property, or for the borrowing of money and pledging of property to secure the payment of the same, and to execute all necessary conveyances pursuant to the direction of the International Executive Committee [1994]).

2. Members of the State Board of Trustees shall hold office until their successors are appointed, and this board shall hold title to manage, and control, or cause to be managed and controlled, pursuant to the direction of the church, all real estate in which the churches or membership of the churches in the state hold a common or general right of interest. These boards shall use the said properties, including, without limitation, campgrounds, state parsonages, and the like, for the sole and exclusive benefit of the Church of God.

3. The said State Board of Trustees shall also hold title to, manage, or cause to be managed and controlled, pursuant to the direction of the Church of God (Cleveland, Tennessee) all real and personal properties in places where no church has been organized (53rd A., 1970, Item 15, pp. 44-46; [1994]).

4. Provided further, that the State Board of Trustees is hereby authorized and empowered, with the consent of the state overseer, to transfer and convey to a Local Board of Trustees, and without a conference of the ministry of the state, such trust property for use of a church, for which such Local Board of Trustees are the trustees (43rd A., 1950, p. 17; [1994]).

5. As directed by the state/regional overseer and state/regional council of the Church of God (Cleveland, Tennessee), the State/Regional Board of Trustees shall have the right to purchase, sell, transfer and convey, or to borrow money and pledge state/regional-owned property to secure the repayment of the same, at any time, provided that the amount involved annually shall not be more than the following schedule:

Category	Amount
5-star	$750,000
4-star	$500,000
AAA	$350,000
AA	$250,000
A	$200,000
Others	as approved by the International Executive Committee

If the amount involved shall be more than the above schedule, then the said proposition or transaction shall be submitted to the International Executive Committee for consideration and, if approved, also to a duly constituted conference of the ministry of the state/region, which will require a two-thirds majority vote for approval. If the said conference shall approve the proposition by a two-thirds majority vote of those attending, then the State/Regional Board of Trustees, with the consent of the state/regional overseer, shall have full power to purchase, sell, hypothecate, transfer and convey any of the said property, or to borrow money and pledge the property for the repayment of the same. (This applies only to the states/regions in the U.S.A. and Canada.) (69th A., 2002, pp. 48, 49)

6. In the case of mission states, approval of the International Executive Committee shall be necessary to borrow money or to encumber the state in any manner (53rd A., 1970, pp. 44-46; 62nd A., 1988, Journal, pp. 49, 50; [1994]).

7. Any person appointed to the State Board of Trustees shall be a member in good standing of the Church of God. If at any time, any member of any Board of Trustees shall cease to be a member in good standing, or if by reason of death, removal, incapacity, or unwillingness to perform all duties of his office, his place on the Board of Trustees may be declared vacant: on the General Board by the general overseer; on a State Board by the state overseer; on a Local Board by a local church conference; and the same authority that declares said office vacant shall appoint a person to serve until the time for regular appointments, and the one so appointed shall have all authority held by the one removed (35th A., 1940, pp. 32-34; [1994]).

S35. STATE BOARD OF MINISTERIAL DEVELOPMENT (57th A., 1978, pp. 37, 38; 64th A., 1992, p. 78)

I. SELECTION

1. Each state shall have a State Board of Ministerial Development.

2. The board and board chairman shall be appointed biennially by the state overseer and approved by the State Council.

3. The board shall consist of not more than five and not less than three members, and may consist of ordained ministers or bishops, and where possible, at least one qualified layperson.

4. The board shall meet as often as the state overseer and chairman deem necessary.

II. DUTIES AND RESPONSIBILITIES

The State Board of Ministerial Development shall:

1. Implement and supervise, under the direction of the state overseer, the educational programs promoted or suggested by the [church].

2. Promote Church of God educational institutions at the state level.

3. Help implement the Ministerial Internship Program.

4. Stimulate and nurture continuing education programs at all levels.

5. Serve in an advisory capacity to churches who sponsor Christian day schools, kindergartens, or day-care centers, or who are in the process of developing such programs.

6. Promote and supervise the Ministerial Development Institutes (MDI).

7. Consult with the state overseer in developing annual regional workshops and seminars for the ministry in areas of Biblical theology, pastoral and personal growth, pastoral administration, counseling, preaching, and such like, in cooperation with the [general church].

8. Work with the Center for Ministerial Care in meeting the needs of ministers and their families.

S36. STATE YOUTH AND DISCIPLESHIP BOARD
(53rd A., 1970, p. 39, p. 41; 67th A., 1998, p. 52; 73rd A., 2010)

I. SELECTION

1. Each state shall have a State Youth and Discipleship Board.

2. The board shall be elected by the ministers of the state.

3. The Board shall consist of not less than three members, who may be either ordained ministers or bishops. In states/regions where the administrative bishop and state council shall determine there are not enough qualified ministers to consider, exhorters who hold credentials with a ministerial file number, and report to state and international headquarters on a monthly basis, shall be considered eligible to serve (72nd A., 2008).

II. DUTIES AND AUTHORITIES

1. The board shall meet as often as the state [Youth and Discipleship] director and state overseer deem necessary.

2. The board shall counsel with and assist the state overseer and state [Youth and Discipleship] director in drafting and promoting a program of Christian education for the local churches in each state, to be ratified by the ministers of the state.

3. The board shall, with the state [Youth and Discipleship] director, plan and conduct a state youth camp (or camps and other state youth activities) as deemed necessary in each respective state.

S37. STATE YOUTH AND DISCIPLESHIP DIRECTOR
(54th A., 1972, pp. 42, 43, 44; 55th A., 1974, p. 53; 56th A., 1976, pp. 48, 49, 55; 69th A., 2002, p. 50; 71st A., 2006, p. 46; 73rd A., 2010; 77th A., 2018).

I. SELECTION

1. The state Youth and Discipleship director shall be nominated by the state overseer and elected by the State Council prior to the International General Assembly.

BOOK OF DISCIPLINE, CHURCH ORDER, AND GOVERNANCE   135

2. The state Youth and Discipleship director's term of office shall be for two years, with a maximum of four consecutive years in a respective non-mission state. [Effective 2020 General Assembly; 77th A., 2018]

3. Credentialed ministers (where practical) shall be used to fill the office.

II. DUTIES AND AUTHORITIES

The state Youth and Discipleship director shall work under the supervision of the state overseer, and the duties and authorities of the Youth and Discipleship director are to be defined by the state overseer and state council (74th A., 2012).

S38. STATE EVANGELISM AND MISSIONS DIRECTOR (USA MISSIONS)

(54th A., 1972, pp. 55, 56; 55th A., 1974, p. 57; 56th A., 1976, pp. 48, 49, 55; 71st A., 2006, p. 46; 73rd A., 2010; 74th A., 2012)

SELECTION

1. The state overseer may submit to the State Council the names of nominees for state Evangelism and Missions director for election prior to the International General Assembly. Ordained bishops (where practical) shall be used to fill the office.

2. The state Evangelism and Missions director's term of office shall be for two years, with a maximum of eight consecutive years in a respective non-mission state.

S39. EVANGELISM PROGRAM

That each state/region establish a Church Planting and Revitalization Task Force and Training Center for the purpose of assessing, coaching, training, and sending church planters, as well as assisting senior pastors to revitalize and grow local congregations, thereby fulfilling the vision and commitment of the Church of God (77th A., 2018).

Each state is to participate in simultaneous revival efforts during the month of October, with a membership emphasis at the conclusion of the revival [1980].

S40. EVANGELISTIC ASSOCIATIONS

Evangelistic associations or other organizations of this type shall not be organized within the Church of God without the express approval of the International Executive Council. All existing organizations shall be either approved by the International Executive Council or be dissolved (50th A., 1964, p. 55).

S41. STATE WORLD MISSIONS BOARD (64th A., 1992, p. 75)

I. SELECTION

1. Each state shall have a State World Missions Board.

2. The board and board chairman shall be appointed biennially by the state overseer.

3. The board shall consist of not more than five and not less than three members. The members shall be ministers or laymen who have shown strong support for world evangelization.

4. The board shall meet as often as the state overseer and chairman deem necessary.

II. DUTIES AND RESPONSIBILITIES

The State World Missions Board shall:

1. Promote world evangelization in the Church of God in the state.

2. Promote state, district, and local world missions conferences, seminars, banquets, and so forth.

3. Assist with the scheduling of field representatives and missionaries on furlough.

S42. STATE MUSIC BOARD (58th A., 1980, p. 37; [1994])

I. SELECTION

1. Each state shall have a State Music Board.

2. The board and board chairman shall be appointed biennially by the state overseer.

3. The board shall consist of not more than five and not less than three members and should consist of ministers, ministers of music, and qualified laymen.

4. The board shall meet as often as the state overseer and chairman deem necessary.

II. DUTIES AND RESPONSIBILITIES

The State Music Board shall:

1. Promote the ministry of music in the Church of God in the state.

2. Implement and supervise, under the direction of the state overseer, the musical programs promoted by the Division of Discipleship Ministries (Worship and Music).

3. Consult with the state overseer in developing state or regional workshops or seminars for ministers of music, choir directors, pianists, organists, and other interested church musicians.

4. Provide a fellowship for church musicians on the state level which will provide for the interchange of information, current trends, and resource materials in church music.

5. Assist in the placement of church musicians when called upon.

6. Assist local churches in establishing and improving their music programs.

7. Periodically study the musical needs and interests of the churches in the state.

S43. DISTRICT OVERSEERS

I. SELECTION

Each district shall be under the care and supervision of a district overseer, appointed by the state overseer.

II. DUTIES AND AUTHORITIES

The district overseer shall:

1. Conduct conferences in each of the churches on his district. However, he may authorize the local pastor to conduct the conference, (65th A., 1994, Item 7, p. 88).

2. See that a general evangelistic effort is put forth in his district during the year.

3. See that the state program is carried out in the churches of his district.

4. Assist the state overseer in the appointment of pastors, when called upon to do so.

5. Together with the state overseer, pass on the selection, purchase, and construction of all church properties on his district.

6. Annually, each district shall identify and participate in a church revitalization project within the district (where feasible) (77th A., 2018).

7. Each district shall be encouraged to establish a goal for church planting every two years in partnership with the state office (77th A., 2018).

S44. DISTRICT YOUTH AND DISCIPLESHIP DIRECTOR (73rd A., 2010)

The district overseer is, by virtue of his office, district Youth and Discipleship director, but if the work requires, the state Youth and Discipleship director, together with the district overseer, may appoint an assistant to serve in this capacity (41st A., 1946, p. 29).

S45. WOMEN'S MINISTRIES (STATE) [WOMEN'S DISCIPLESHIP]

(50th A., 1964, p. 65; 53rd A., 1970, p. 43; 59th A., 1982, p. 43; 67th A., 1998, p. 52; 73rd A., 2010); [2014]

I. Purpose and Objectives

To facilitate this ministry each state shall institute whatever means they deem advisable in keeping with the declared purposes of the Church of God.

II. President

1. The office of Church of God Women's Discipleship president [at the state level] shall be created.

2. The wife of the state overseer shall fill this office.

3. The purpose of this office shall be to provide leadership for Women's Discipleship [at the state level] in cooperation with the general church program [1982].

CHURCH GOVERNMENT—
LOCAL
(S46 through S65)

S46. RELATIONSHIP OF LOCAL CHURCH TO THE INTERNATIONAL GENERAL ASSEMBLY
(58th A., 1980, pp. 38, 39; [1994]).

1. The Church of God (Cleveland, Tennessee, U.S.A.) has a centralized (by legal definition "hierarchical") form of church government. The International General Assembly, the highest authority of the Church of God, governs the ownership of all church property, both real and personal. All property is held in trust for members composing said International General Assembly. The local churches, the names of which are officially registered with the Church of God, Cleveland, Tennessee, U.S.A. are the results of the faithful services of the ministers and representatives of the International General Assembly; and these churches, when thus received by the representatives of the International General Assembly, then become and compose constituents of the International General Assembly. Therefore, the right of any local church as a whole to withdraw from the International General Assembly is not recognized and does not exist, but those members who prove disloyal to the government and teachings as promulgated from time to time by the International General Assembly, or who are otherwise disorderly, are to be dealt with as individuals.

2. The International General Assembly of the Church of God (Cleveland, Tennessee, U.S.A.) is that organized body with full power and authority to designate the teachings, principles, and practices of all the local churches composing said Assembly.

3. The International General Assembly governs the operation (including ownership of all real and personal property) of the Church of God, Cleveland, Tennessee, U.S.A., at all structural levels: international, national, state/territorial, district, and local. The International General Assembly has vested in the office of the state overseer authority over the local churches. Some of his powers, all of which are more fully explained elsewhere in this book of *Minutes*, can be exercised to remove pastors, to appoint pastors, or a special Board of Trustees, which may be the State Board of Trustees, to hold title to local property.

4. A Local Board of Trustees shall hold title to, manage, and control, pursuant to the direction of the local congregation, all real estate owned by the local congregation by which they are selected, provided that all such property shall be used, managed, and

controlled for the sole and exclusive use and benefit of the Church of God, Cleveland, Tennessee, U.S.A. In the event that the majority or all of the local church depart from the faith or discontinue fellowship with the organization, the state overseer shall at any time have power to appoint other trustees to hold the property for the Church of God.

5. Local churches, when they have been accepted into the Church of God, are therefore bound by the decisions of the International General Assembly in matters of doctrine, teaching, and polity.

S47. LOCAL CHURCH DEVELOPMENT PLAN
(72nd A., 2008)

A Local Church Development Plan shall be implemented by the International Executive Committee, in conjunction with each respective state/regional overseer, for the purpose of increasing the effectiveness of local churches in the fulfillment of their mission, through a plan designed to involve lay leadership, together with pastoral oversight, for church growth in the twenty-first century.

This shall be a standardized plan designed to meet the needs of local churches at each numerical level.

S48. MEMBERS (45th A., 1954, p. 27; 61st A., 1986, p. 54; 68th A., 2000, p. 83)

I. Procedure for Receiving Members Into the Church
A. Church Membership

Church membership is Scriptural, and any person presenting himself as a prospective member is making a serious and far-reaching decision. It is the responsibility of the pastor to see that all persons making themselves available for membership are fully informed of the doctrine, teachings, government, and heritage of the Church of God. In keeping with this responsibility, the pastor shall inform all persons presenting themselves for membership through one or more of the following ways:

1. Counsel with prospective members privately concerning the membership requirements and their responsibilities to them.

2. Conduct special membership classes where prospective members are taught membership requirements.

3. Read and explain the membership requirements in a public meeting.

B. Procedure for Receiving Members

Following this [the foregoing] procedure, the minister shall invite prospective members to stand before the altar and face the congregation. The minister shall then proceed by giving the following charge to the applicants as he stands before them.

1. You realize in presenting yourself for membership that you are assuming a solemn obligation, and it is expected that you will always be true to your promise and faithfully fulfill and discharge your obligation as a loyal member.

2. Do you publicly confess and testify that you know the Lord Jesus Christ as your personal Savior in the full pardon of your sins? (The applicant(s) will answer, I do.)

3. Are you willing to walk in the light of the Scripture as it shines upon your path? (I am.)

4. Are you willing to abide by and subscribe to the discipline of the Church of God as outlined by the Scripture and set forth in the Minutes of the International General Assembly? (I am.)

5. Are you willing to support the church with your attendance and temporal means to the best of your ability as the Lord prospers you? (I am.)

6. Do you agree to be subject to the counsel and admonition of those who are over you in the Lord? (I do.)

7. If there be any member who has a legal objection to any of these becoming members of the Church of God, the objector may now so state.

8. By the authority vested in me as a minister of the Church of God, I take great pleasure in welcoming you into this membership and extending to you the right hand of fellowship. May I encourage you to call for the services of your pastor when needed.

9. I have confidence that you will ever be a faithful member and a blessing to the church and that the church will be a blessing to you. I pray our fellowship will always be bound together with unbroken love. (The minister shall then pray.)

C. Instructions

It would be well to have a musical background while the church gives the right hand of fellowship.

It is believed that friends of the church should be extended the privilege of bidding the new members Godspeed in like manner (45th A., 1954, p. 27).

II. LOCAL CHURCH LEADERSHIP (65th A., 1994, Item 4, p. 86)

We affirm the Scriptural pattern of elders and deacons (Acts 6:1-7; 1 Timothy 3:1-13; 4:14; 2 Timothy 2:2; Titus 1:6-9) and every local congregation, in consultation with the state and territorial overseers, is encouraged to implement this Scriptural pattern of leadership.

Further, the International Executive Committee shall make available quality resources to assist overseers and pastors in the implementation of this Scriptural pattern.

III. Local Church Part of the Assembly

1. The local churches, the names of which are officially registered with the Church of God, Cleveland, Tennessee, U.S.A., are the result of the faithful services of the ministers and representatives of the International General Assembly; and these churches, when thus received by the representatives of the International General Assembly, then became and composed a part of the International General Assembly. Therefore, the right of any local church as a whole to withdraw from the International General Assembly is not recognized and does not exist, but those members who prove disloyal to the government and teachings as promulgated from time to time by the International General Assembly, or who are otherwise disorderly, are to be dealt with as individuals (15th A., 1920, p. 50; 45th A., 1954, pp. 27, 28; 50th A., 1964, p. 54).

2. If a church is organized and they do not accept the teachings of the International General Assembly, they cannot be recognized by headquarters [at any level of church government] as a Church of God (15th A., 1920, p. 68).

IV. Requirements of Members

A. Exclusion for Nonattendance

Members should be excluded from the Church of God for nonattendance of the regular services of the church of which they are members, unless they have a good reason. Notice the question is only for continued nonattendance; this doesn't mean just for a few times missing service (20th A., 1925, p. 41).

B. Stand Against Gambling

Inasmuch as the Church of God believes gambling to be contrary to Christian principle and practice; and

Inasmuch as there has been a tendency to compromise among some states and churches, teaching that state lotteries, bingo games, games of chance, and so forth, are not contrary to present Christian moral standards; therefore

The Church of God continues its stated opposition to the evils of gambling and urges its people to exhibit by precept and example its belief in the high standards of holiness conduct required of all believers (50th A., 1964, p. 55).

C. Holy Living and Modesty

"Love not the world, neither the things that are in the world. If any man love the world, the love of the Father is not in him. For all that is in the world, the lust of the flesh, and the lust of the eyes, and the pride of life, is not of the Father, but is of the world" (1 John 2:15, 16).

"In like manner also, that women adorn themselves in modest apparel, with shamefacedness and sobriety not with broided hair, or gold, or pearls, or costly array" (1 Timothy 2:9).

"Whose adorning let it not be that outward adorning of plaiting the hair, and of wearing of gold, or of putting on of apparel; but let it be the hidden man of the heart, in that which is not corruptible, even the ornament of a meek and quiet spirit, which is in the sight of God of great price" (1 Peter 3:3, 4) (35th A., 1940, p. 31; 66th A., 1996, p. 61).

V. LOCAL CHURCH AND RETIRED MINISTERS (70th A., 2004 p. 58)

That each local church establish a program to "Adopt a Retired Church of God Minister," recognizing them on special days of their lives (i.e. birthdays, anniversaries, hospitalizations) and assisting them financially when they are invited to speak or on aforementioned occasions.

S49. MEMBERSHIP

I. TRANSFER OF MEMBERSHIP

1. When a member in good standing moves from the vicinity of one church to another, a letter of recommendation should be given on request, in harmony with [the scripture] "I commend unto you Phebe our sister, which is a servant of the church which is at Cenchrea: that ye receive her in the Lord, as becometh saints" (Romans 16:1, 2) (1st A., 1906, Bk. Min, p. 18).

2. Inasmuch as we live in a mobile society which affects many of the constituents of the church, it is important that pastors and leaders show care and concern in assisting members in relocating, by making available to them information relative to the churches in the area to which they are moving.

3. A member's name should remain on the membership roll until an official request for transfer is received (64th A., 1992, p. 77).

4. Requests for transfers should be granted within two weeks, when requested by the proper authorities, providing no charges are pending. Transfers may be granted or members' transfers may be received at any regular church service (46th A., 1956, p. 24).

5. Inasmuch as the Full Gospel Church of God in South Africa is a part of the Church of God in America, it should be understood that the transfer of membership between local churches of the respective countries is reciprocal; but in no case is it legal to retain local church membership in both countries (46th A., 1956, p. 23).

II. Associate Membership Not Permitted

Inasmuch as the local Church of God membership is composed of Christians who have accepted the teachings, doctrines, and government of the Church of God, and who have been formally received into its fellowship; therefore, no local church has authority to set up or recognize an associate membership of Christians who, for some reason, have not been formally received into its fellowship (45th A., 1954, p. 28).

III. Membership Roll

The pastor and church treasurer shall maintain an accurate, up-to-date membership roll, staying in contact with members who are unable to attend church regularly and members who are in the Armed Forces, encouraging them to attend and transfer their membership to a local Church of God or Ministry to the Military Center in the area where they are stationed (63rd A., 1990, p. 78).

IV. Excluded Members

1. Individuals who have been excluded from any local church shall not be admitted to membership in any other local church until fellowship has been established in business session with the church from which they were excluded. And if the church has been disbanded where he/she was a member, his/her case must be passed on by the state overseer of the state where he/she was excluded and the district overseer where he/she now lives.

2. In case excluded members are put forward by those in authority, such as being used as Sunday school teachers, or otherwise given prominence in the church, especially over protest of the church that excluded them, such action shall be considered disloyalty and all those who do such should be dealt with accordingly (29th A., 1934, p. 56).

V. Procedure in Dealing With Member

If a member who is not a minister shall be charged with any offense which makes it necessary to deal with the member, formal charges in writing shall be given to the member not less than three days (when practical) prior to the time and place of the meeting. The member shall have a right to be heard and offer corroborating testimony at the meeting. Further, the charges shall be heard and a decision rendered by the local church and pastor's council or (if a church does not have a pastor's council or board of elders) by the members who are present at the meeting and in good standing with the church. Disciplinary options include but are not limited to: official reprimand, restitution, censure, restrictions, and, where necessary, excommunication (74th A., 2012).

In those cases in which he deems it in the best interests of the local church to do so, the state/regional overseer shall have the authority to excommunicate an unruly or uncooperative member without a formal hearing. A member disfellowshipped by a state/regional overseer shall have the right to appeal to the International Executive Committee within 10 days of the written notice of the overseer's action. The decision of the International Executive Committee is final, with no further recourse for appeal by the member. The local church must remove the member's name from the membership roll when notified of the action by the state overseer (71st A., 2006, p. 48).

VI. Right to Appeal

If the member is not satisfied with the decision of the conference, he/she may appeal. The complainant must, within ten (10) days, notify the state overseer (in writing) the reasons for dissatisfaction. In such case, the church treasurer and pastor must furnish the state overseer the full information (in writing) of the business meeting in which the member was excluded.

The state overseer shall have power to make the final decision in the matter of the appeal. If in his judgment the case warrants calling a state board, he may do so. In either case there shall be no further appeal.

In the event the appeal is sustained, the state overseer shall notify the pastor and treasurer in writing of the decision, and instructions shall be that the pastor or treasurer read the letter to the members in a called meeting. If the appeal hearing results in clearing the member of formal charges, he/she shall be reinstated in good standing without delay.

When a member wishes his/her membership dropped from the roll of a local church, his/her request shall be made in writing to the pastor, with a copy to the treasurer. His/her request shall be granted by the church in conference, provided he/she has been a loyal member and there are no charges pending. Since this action will have been instigated by the member, he/she needs no notification (31st A., 1936, p. 34; 38th A., 1943, p. 30; 42nd A., 1948, p. 29; 54th A., 1972, p. 53).

S50. CONFERENCES

I. PURPOSE

A church conference is a business meeting for the purpose of transacting any business necessary for the operation of the local church (65th A., 1994, Item 7, p. 88).

II. WHO MAY CONDUCT A CONFERENCE

1. No pastor has the right to hold a conference without permission from the district overseer (22nd A., 1927, p. 32; 46th A., 1956, p. 25; 54th A., 1972, p. 54).

2. No conference shall be held in the district except under the direction or supervision of the district overseer. This does not exclude the authority of the overseer of the state, which is fully explained in the *Minutes* of the International General Assembly (13th A., 1917, p. 36).

3. In any instance where there is not a sufficient number of active members in the local church to assist in conducting a conference, the state or district overseer, and two or more ministers whom he may select, shall make full disposition of all matters that may demand attention.

4. The state and district overseers should see that at least one conference a year is conducted in each local church in their respective state or territory (37th A., 1942, p. 36; 65th A., 1994, Item 7, p. 88).

5. The local church has a right to appoint a committee in conference to look after some affairs of the church. Such a committee, however, is to do nothing that would conflict with or violate the local, state, and general church program and government, or create confusion (46th A., 1956, pp. 25, 26).

III. REGULAR CONFERENCE

1. The regular conference, consisting of the membership, is called or set for any regularly designated time by the pastor or

district overseer. The purpose of the conference is to inform the church of its financial status. The church conference shall also consider any other business referred to it by the pastor and his church council. All major disbursements must be approved by the church in conference.

2. The regular conference should be announced at least ten (10) days before it is to occur.

IV. CALLED CONFERENCE

1. The called conference consists of all members of the local church who wish to attend, said conference to convene at a time set by the pastor to take care of business arising between the regular conferences. This does not exclude the rights of the state and district overseers to call or moderate conferences in local churches (65th A., 1994, Item 7, p. 88).

2. When it is necessary to have a called conference, all members of the local church should be notified if possible (46th A., 1954, p. 32).

V. ORDER OF CONFERENCES

Robert's Rules of Order Newly Revised shall serve as the guide for conducting all business conferences.

Usual order of business:

1. Financial reports of various departments of the church
2. Other reports of committees, and so forth
3. Transfer of membership, if any
4. Unfinished business left from previous meeting
5. New business

S51. PASTOR

I. APPOINTMENT OF PASTORS

1. The authority for the appointment of pastors is vested in the state overseer (45th A., 1954, p. 34; 51st A., 1966, p. 59).

2. Local churches are to refrain from taking action on the selection of pastors until authorized to do so by the state overseer (28th A., 1933, p. 38).

3. The state overseer shall appoint the pastor subsequent to consultation with the district overseer, and after having given members of the local church an opportunity to express themselves regarding their desire for pastor of their choice (61st A., 1986, p. 53).

4. The state overseer may call for an expression from the membership (at least 16 years of age) when there is an apparent decline in the spiritual health and well-being of the local church (61st A., 1986, p. 53).

5. The signature [of the individual expressing a pastoral preference] is required on the local church uniform pastoral preference ballot (49th A., 1962, p. 53).

PASTORAL PREFERENCE EXPRESSION

Name of church _____

Are you a member of this local church?	☐ Yes	☐ No
Do you attend services regularly?	☐ Yes	☐ No
Do you pay tithes regularly to this church?	☐ Yes	☐ No
Do you recommend a pastoral change?	☐ Yes	☐ No

If yes, whom do you recommend for pastor?

_____

Signature _____

II. Procedure for Effecting a Pastoral Change

When a pastor desires a pastoral change, he/she shall submit a letter of request to the state overseer, who shall keep this request in strictest confidence, except with those involved in the placement process (61st A., 1986, p. 53).

III. Procedure for Laity Contacting State Overseer

The state overseer serves both the ministry and laity; therefore, when loyal, tithing members of a local church have a legitimate concern as it relates to the welfare of their church, they have the right and privilege to contact their state overseer, after they have contacted their pastor and district overseer. All concerns expressed to the state overseer should be communicated to the pastor and district overseer with the names of the individuals expressing such concerns. These concerns should be preferably in writing, not as part of a petition (63rd A., 1990, p. 76).

IV. Assistant Pastor

Where assistant pastors are needed, they are to be nominated by the local church and pastor, subject to the approval and appointment of the state overseer (44th A., 1952, p. 31; 74th A., 2012).

V. REFORMATION SUNDAY OFFERING

The pastor of each local church shall set aside Reformation Sunday (the last Sunday in October) annually in honor of aged ministers for the purpose of raising a special love offering, said receipts to be sent to the Church of God Secretary General (64th A., 1992, B., 3., p. 247).

S52. CHURCH AND PASTOR'S COUNCIL

(34th A., 1934, p. 22; 50th A., 1964, pp. 57, 58; 51st A., 1966, p. 60; 56th A., 1976, pp. 50, 51; 73rd A., 2010)

I. SELECTION

1. When a local church deems it practical to have a Church and Pastor's Council, said council shall be elected by the governing body of the church consisting of the loyal members. Members of the Church and Pastor's Council shall be loyal members of the church.

2. This council is to be elected biennially and by ballot.

3. A system of rotation may be used whereby council members will serve a designated length of time.

4. In the event the office of one of the council members is vacated between elections because the incumbent dies, becomes disabled, or is in any other way disqualified, the pastor is to submit to the governing body of the local church the names of the two individuals who received the next highest number of votes in the last election, so that one may be selected to fill the vacancy. Alternates may be elected during the regular election to fill any vacancies.

II. SIZE AND CHAIRMANSHIP

The number on the Church and Pastor's Council shall be:

Membership up to 100, not less than three (3) councilors.
Membership 101-225, not less than five (5) councilors.
Membership 226-350, not less than seven (7) councilors.
Membership 351-500, not less than nine (9) councilors.
Membership 501 and over, not less than twelve (12) councilors.

The pastor shall serve as chairman of the Church and Pastor's Council, shall call all regular monthly or quarterly meetings, and may call special meetings as needed. No meeting shall be called without the permission of the pastor, district overseer, or state overseer.

III. Qualifications for Church and Pastor's Council

"Wherefore, brethren, look ye out among you seven men of honest report, full of the Holy Ghost and wisdom, whom we may appoint over this business" (Acts 6:3).

A member who serves on the Church and Pastor's Council must be:
1. A loyal member of the church, adhering to its teachings.
2. Baptized in the Holy Ghost.
3. Faithful in tithing.
4. A regular church attendant.
5. One who works in harmony with the local, state, and general church's program and reflects a cooperative attitude toward the progress of the church.

IV. Duties and Responsibilities

1. The Church and Pastor's Council, under the direction of the pastor, shall promote the general and state outreach programs of the church.

2. The Church and Pastor's Council shall work in harmony with the pastor and assist him/her, when called upon, in the institution and direction of the local church program in the following areas:

Spiritual
The Church and Pastor's Council, under the direction of the pastor, shall encourage spiritual growth of the local congregation with emphasis on personal Bible reading, prayer, family devotions, tithing and giving, Christian service, and personal witnessing.

Financial
The Church and Pastor's Council, under the direction of the pastor, shall approve the disbursement of church funds. (This does not include Women's Ministries monies.) All major disbursements must be approved by the church in conference. Each congregation shall determine what amount constitutes a major disbursement.

Physical
The Church and Pastor's Council, under the direction of the pastor, shall provide and maintain proper building facilities for the congregation and a proper residence for the pastor. The council shall see that all church properties are properly insured and tax-exempt, when the secular government provides such exemption.

S53. CHURCH TREASURER

(1st A., 1906, Bk. Min, p. 15; 13th A., 1917, Bk. Min, pp. 19, 286; 24th A., 1929, p. 23; 30th A., 1935, p. 36; 45th A., 1954, p. 26; 49th A., 1962, p. 33; 50th A., 1964, p. 58; 51st A., 1966, p. 60; 55th A., 1974, p. 54; 56th A., 1976, pp. 51, 52; [1976]; 65th A., 1994, Item 10, p. 89; 68th A., 2000, p. 82).

I. SELECTION

1. A church treasurer shall be appointed by the pastor and confirmed by the council and/or the church body.

2. The church treasurer or a member of the council may serve as recording secretary of the Church and Pastor's Council.

3. Each local church is to provide the treasurer with a copy of the current *Minutes* of the International General Assembly. An adequate bookkeeping system is to be used in all churches [2018].

II. QUALIFICATIONS OF CHURCH TREASURER

To serve as church treasurer one must be:

1. A loyal member of the church, adhering to its teachings.

2. Baptized in the Holy Ghost.

3. Faithful in tithing.

4. A regular church attendant.

5. One who performs duties under the supervision of the pastor and with his approval.

6. One who works in harmony with the church's program and reflects a cooperative attitude with reference to the progress of the local church.

7. Any exceptions to the above qualifications must be approved by the state overseer.

III. DUTIES AND RESPONSIBILITIES OF CHURCH TREASURER

The church treasurer shall:

1. Determine and maintain an accurate record of the date of the organization of the church and all other vital information pertaining to the local church organization.

2. Keep an accurate record of the names and addresses of all local church members.

3. Report monthly to the secretary general, on MAP (Moving Active Pentecostals) ministry forms, the names and addresses of all members moving from their local church to another area.

BOOK OF DISCIPLINE, CHURCH ORDER, AND GOVERNANCE 153

4. Record and maintain accurate minutes of all church conferences and business transactions (loans, property transactions, and so forth).

5. Maintain an accurate record of all the local church conferences and disbursements, at the church, where possible.

6. Prepare monthly reports and send one copy to the secretary general and one copy to the state overseer by the fifth of each month on the [reporting] forms provided by the secretary general's office.

7. Prepare a financial report for each quarterly conference.

8. Furnish an itemized list of all receipts and disbursements to the pastor each week.

9. Disburse money from the church treasury under the direction of the pastor. (The pastor and treasurer are to sign all authorized checks.)

S54. FINANCIAL SYSTEM
(25th A., 1930, p. 21; 45th A., 1954, p. 32; 56th A., 1976, p. 53; 62nd A, 1988, Journal, p. 50; 65th A., 1994, Item 5, p. 86; 72nd A., 2008; [2010]).

I. FINANCE COMMITTEE

Because of an ever-increasing responsibility upon those handling money in the local churches, each church is to have a Finance Committee.

A. Selection

The Finance Committee shall consist of the treasurer and two other members. The second and third members shall be appointed by the pastor and confirmed by the Church and Pastor's Council and/or the members of the church (70th A., 2004 p. 56).

B. Qualifications of Finance Committee Members

A member of the Finance Committee must be:

1. A loyal member of the church, adhering to its teachings.
2. Baptized in the Holy Ghost.
3. Faithful in tithing.
4. A regular church attendant.
5. One who works in harmony with the church's programs and reflects a cooperative attitude with reference to the progress of the local church.
6. Any exceptions to the above qualifications must be approved by the state overseer.

C. **Duties and Responsibilities of the Finance Committee**
The Finance Committee shall:
1. Receive and count all monies.
2. Prepare funds for deposit.

II. TITHING

1. All members and ministers of the Church of God shall pay tithes into the church where they are members.

Percentage of Tithes Paid Into the Local Church
To Be Sent to International Office and State/Regional Office

Local church treasurers shall send a percentage of tithes paid into the local church to the International Office (secretary general) with their monthly report, and an equal amount to their State/Regional Office (state treasurer) with their monthly report as follows, with the remainder for the support of the pastor (72nd A., 2008; [2010]).

After September 1, 2014   5%   To International Office
                           5%   To State/Regional Office

Note: For breakdown of percentage division of amount sent to the secretary general for International Office and World Missions, see page 83 in this book.

2. Surplus tithes are to be used for the benefit of the ministry as may be decided by the state overseer, pastor, and local church, and churches having surplus tithes are encouraged to sponsor a work in a new field within the state, or in some mission state or territory. Each new work in a mission state or territory, sponsored by a local church, shall be under the direction of the respective state overseer and local church sponsoring such work. A monthly report of the progress of the new work shall be furnished to the sponsoring church (33rd A., 1938, pp. 50, 51; 36th A., 1941, p. 48; 38th A., 1943, p. 30; 45th A., 1954, p. 29; [1986]).

III. CHURCH REPORTS (65th A., 1994, Item 6, pp. 86-88)

A. **Consistency in Reporting**
The principle of local churches giving a tithe of their tithe for worldwide ministry has been a part of Church of God practice from its earliest days. As a Scriptural principle (Genesis 14:18-20; 28:20-22; Malachi 3:10; Luke 11:42; 1 Corinthians 9:6-9; 16:2; Hebrews 7:1-21) and an approved program of the International General Assembly,

tithing the tithe provides a way for each local church to have a part in contributing to the worldwide ministry of the church. Through faithfulness and consistency in this practice, the local church extends its ministry far beyond its own borders and releases God's blessing in the same way that a church member's practice of tithing brings blessings into his/her personal life.

Where there is delinquency in local church reporting (reports and/or finances), the following procedures are recommended:

1. When a church is two months delinquent in reporting, the state overseer shall meet personally with the pastor, relative to correcting the matter.

2. When the church is three months delinquent, a board of inquiry shall be appointed to investigate and make recommendations.

3. Should the delinquency continue, a state board shall be appointed to consider the filing of appropriate charges.

4. Where the foregoing investigation has proven fault on the part of a pastor, that he not be considered for any appointment or position until proper disposition has been made for payment of the delinquent funds.

5. Further, any pastor who is found at fault by an investigation committee, who has failed to send in his/her respective church reports for four (4) months or more, shall be subject to disciplinary action from his/her respective Administrative Bishop, up to revocation of credentials. The Administrative Bishop can make exceptions to this ruling on a case-by-case basis, and as is in compliance with the *Minutes* of the General Assembly, **S7. Section II, Paragraph 11,** under **Duties of the General Overseer.** The action of the Administrative Bishop must be approved by the general overseer of the Church of God (the Presiding Bishop) for final determination (77th A., 2018).

B. **Accumulated Delinquent Funds**

The state overseer is required to fully inform any pastoral candidate of the current financial condition of the prospective church prior to finalization of said candidate's appointment.

Where there has been an accumulation of delinquent funds from a local church for which the present pastor is not responsible, the following procedures are recommended:
1. That the state overseer or a committee appointed by him shall meet with the current pastor to study the situation and make recommendations for an appropriate resolution of the problem according to one of the following options:
   - Immediate payment
   - Payment plan
   - Partial payment and partial assistance
   - Full assistance be given when the above options have been exercised and it is beyond the ability of the local church to satisfy the delinquent debt within a maximum of 12 months.

NOTE: There is no provision for forgiveness of ministry money owed. However, assistance may be provided through funds being made available by (1) an individual, (2) another local church, (3) the state office, (4) international headquarters, or any combination of the above.

2.. When all other sources for payment of the delinquent amount have been exhausted, the state overseer shall have the right to appeal to the secretary general with a proposal providing for mutual participation in the payment of the accumulated delinquent funds. Further, that a standing committee of action chaired by the secretary general be appointed by the general overseer to consider and make final disposition of such proposals.

S55. CHURCH PROPERTY
(35th A., 1940, p. 30; 46th A., 1956, p. 24; 63rd A., 1990, pp. 78, 79; [1994])

I. CENTRALIZED FORM OF GOVERNMENT

The Church of God (Cleveland, Tennessee, U.S.A.) has a centralized (by legal definition "hierarchical") form of church government. The International General Assembly, the highest authority of the Church of God, governs the ownership of all church property, both real and personal. All property is held in trust for members composing said International General Assembly [1994].

II. AUTHORITY OF THE INTERNATIONAL GENERAL ASSEMBLY

The International General Assembly of the Church of God (Cleveland, Tennessee, U.S.A.) is that organized body with full power and authority to designate the teaching, government, principles and practices of all the local churches composing said Assembly [1994].

1. The International General Assembly governs the operation (including ownership of all real and personal property) of the Church of God (Cleveland, Tennessee, U.S.A.) at all structural levels: international, national, state/territorial, district, and local.

2. Local churches, the names of which are officially registered with the Church of God, Cleveland, Tennessee, U.S.A., are the result of the faithful services of the ministers and representatives of the International General Assembly; and these churches, when thus received by the representatives of the International General Assembly, then become and compose a part of the International General Assembly. Therefore, the right of any local church as a whole to withdraw from the International General Assembly is not recognized and does not exist, but those members who prove disloyal to the government and teachings as promulgated from time to time by the International General Assembly, or who are otherwise disorderly, are to be dealt with as individuals.

III. POLITY AND PROPERTY

Believing a centralized form of government to be the Biblical (Acts 15:13–29) standard for our churches, the Church of God (Cleveland, Tennessee, U.S.A.) early adopted such a form of government and has consistently practiced a centralized form of government [1994].

Therefore:

1. The polity of the Church of God (Cleveland, Tennessee, U.S.A.) regarding both real and personal property ownership directly reflects the religious conviction that a centralized (by legal definition "hierarchical") form of government is Biblically mandated.

2. Title to all real and personal property now owned or hereafter acquired by the Church of God (Cleveland, Tennessee, U.S.A.) at any structural level shall be held by and/or conveyed and transferred to its duly elected or appointed trustees and their

successors in office in trust for the use and benefit of the Church of God (Cleveland, Tennessee, U.S.A.). Every instrument of conveyance of real estate shall contain the appropriate trust clauses under the caption "Deeds" as set forth in Section V below.

3. No state, council, board, agency, local church, individual, or other entity of a local Church of God can financially obligate the Church of God (Cleveland, Tennessee, U.S.A.) without prior written specific consent from the International Executive Committee.

IV. ALL PROPERTY OWNED IN TRUST FOR CHURCH OF GOD (CLEVELAND, TENNESSEE)

Title to all properties held at general or state/territorial level, or by a local church, shall be held in trust for the Church of God (Cleveland, Tennessee, U.S.A.) subject to the provisions outlined in the International General Assembly *Minutes*. Should any member or members, in whole or in part, decide to withdraw from the Church of God (Cleveland, Tennessee, U.S.A.), or to take action contrary to the polity of the Church of God (Cleveland, Tennessee, U.S.A.), it is understood that the ownership of all property, both real and personal, remains with the Church of God (Cleveland, Tennessee, U.S.A.) [1994].

V. STANDARD DEEDS RECOGNIZING TRUST OWNERSHIP [1994]

In order to secure the right of property, real and personal, care shall be taken that all conveyances and deeds be drawn and executed in due conformity to the laws of the respective states, provinces and countries in which the property is situated, and also consistent with the International General Assembly *Minutes'* provisions that property is held in trust for the Church of God (Cleveland, Tennessee, U.S.A.). All deeds or other written instruments by which properties are held or hereafter acquired for the use and benefit of the Church of God (Cleveland, Tennessee, U.S.A.) shall contain one of the following applicable statements:

1. To have and to hold by the General Board of Trustees and their successors in trust; for the exclusive use and benefit of the Church of God, Cleveland, Tennessee, U.S.A.

2. To have and to hold by the State/Territorial Board of Trustees and their successors in trust; for the exclusive use and benefit of the Church of God, Cleveland, Tennessee, U.S.A.

3. To have and to hold by the Local Board of Trustees of the local Church of God (their names are to be recorded on the deed) and their successors in trust; for the exclusive use and benefit of the Church of God, Cleveland, Tennessee. The deeds for all local church property shall also contain each of the following clauses:

A. The said Local Board of Trustees shall have full right, power and authority to sell, exchange, transfer and convey said property or to borrow money and pledge the said real estate for the repayment of the same and to execute all necessary deeds, conveyances, and so forth, provided the proposition shall first be presented to a regular or called conference of the said local church, presided over and approved by the state or territorial overseer of the Church of God (Cleveland, Tennessee, U.S.A.), or one whom he may appoint, and the project approved by two–thirds of all members of the said local congregation present and voting. Certification is to be given in writing by the state/territorial overseer that this transaction is in the best interest of the Church of God (Cleveland, Tennessee, U.S.A.), provided that he approves such action [1994].

B. If the local congregation at the place above described shall at any time cease to function or exist, or shall act contrary to Church of God polity, or separate from the Church of God (Cleveland, Tennessee, U.S.A.), then said trustees shall hold title to said real estate, including personal property, for the Church of God (Cleveland, Tennessee, U.S.A.) generally in the state where said real estate is located; and said trustees shall convey the said real estate upon demand to the State Board of Trustees of the Church of God (Cleveland, Tennessee, U.S.A.) in said state, which said state board shall be authorized to use said real estate and personal property, or the proceeds derived from the sale of same (said state board being authorized to sell and convey the said real estate and personal property at any time after title is vested in it), for the use and benefit of the Church of God (Cleveland, Tennessee, U.S.A.) in that state generally; or the founding of another Church of God (Cleveland, Tennessee, U.S.A.) in the same state, or for the promotion of one already existing [1994].

C. If at any time the Local Board of Trustees shall cease to exist or perform its duties for any reason, then the state overseer of the state in which said real estate is located shall have the authority to declare all offices on the said board vacant, and the State Board of Trustees of the Church of God for that state shall automatically then hold title to said property as evidenced by an appropriate instrument filed in the local county register of deeds [1994].

D. The limitations set forth herein are those appearing in the *Minutes* of the International General Assembly of the Church of God most currently in effect, and said *Minutes* are expressly incorporated herein by reference [1994].

4. Standard Church of God Warranty Deed Forms are available from the International Offices of the Church of God (Cleveland, Tennessee, U.S.A.) and should be used whenever practical. The standard Church of God Warranty Deed (printed form) shall contain the essential language recited in Section V, Item 3, A–D above, as amended from time to time by the International General Assembly. Printed standard Church of God Warranty Deed forms dated prior to 1994 are sufficient as they likewise establish the ownership of local church properties in an express trust for the Church of God (Cleveland, Tennessee, U.S.A.).

VI. REGISTRATION OF DEEDS [1994]

All deeds shall be registered or recorded directly upon their execution in their respective county courthouses. Copies of the executed deeds for general, state, and local properties shall be maintained as follows:

General properties—office of the secretary general

State properties—office of the state/territorial secretary-treasurer

Local properties—offices of the state/territorial overseer and local church treasurer

Before any deed is recorded, it is to have the written approval of the proper person: general properties, by the secretary general; state and local properties, by the state or territorial overseer.

VII. INSURANCE

Pastors and churches are required to keep all property under their care adequately insured where practical (38th A., 1943, p. 30).

VIII. CHURCH LEGAL LIABILITY (65th A., 1994, Item 9, p. 89)

Inasmuch as the National Child Care Act of 1993 has direct legal impact and implications with regard to ministry to minors, it is recommended that all church pastors, staff ministers, church leaders, and volunteer workers be informed of the general statement of the law. Further, since state laws regarding child abuse differ from state to state, it is imperative that all church pastors, staff ministers, church leaders, and volunteer workers make a thorough study of respective state laws and take all necessary steps for compliance and legal safeguard.

S56. LOCAL BOARD OF TRUSTEES [1994]

I. SELECTION

Each local church or congregation that owns any property (either real or personal), shall appoint a Local Board of Trustees, to consist of not less than three members, said board to be selected by the local congregation in a business meeting.

II. DUTIES AND AUTHORITIES

1. Members of the Local Board of Trustees shall hold office until their successors are appointed. The Local Board of Trustees shall hold title to, manage and control, pursuant to the direction of the local congregation, not inconsistent with the International General Assembly *Minutes*, all real estate and personal property owned by the local congregation by which they are selected, provided that all such property shall be used, managed, and controlled for the sole and exclusive use and benefit of the Church of God (Cleveland, Tennessee, U.S.A.).

2. The said Local Board of Trustees shall have full right, power, and authority to buy property for the use or benefit of the local congregation; to sell, hypothecate, exchange, transfer, and convey any of the local property held by it, or to borrow money and pledge the said property for the repayment of the same; and to execute all necessary deeds, conveyances, and so forth, provided that each of the following conditions is met: (1) the proposition shall first be presented to a regular or called conference of the local church; (2) presided over by the state overseer, or one whom he may appoint; (3) approved by a two-thirds majority vote; and (4) provided further that the board have a certification, in writing, from the state overseer, or one whom he may appoint, that the proposition is not adverse to the interest of the Church of God (Cleveland, Tennessee, U.S.A.).

3. If any local church shall cease to function or exist, or remain in good standing with the Church of God (Cleveland, Tennessee, U.S.A.), then the Local Board of Trustees shall hold the local property, both real and personal, in trust for the Church of God (Cleveland, Tennessee, U.S.A.) generally in the state or territory where located, and said local board shall convey the local property

as directed by the state/territorial overseer to the state/territorial Board of Trustees, to be used and disposed of by it for the use and benefit of the church in that state/territory generally; or said state/territorial board may use the said property, or the proceeds derived from the sale of the same, for the founding of another church in the state/territory, or the promotion of one already existing.

III. REMOVAL/REPLACEMENT

1. If the Local Board of Trustees has ceased to exist or perform its duties, then the state overseer shall have the authority to declare all offices thereon vacant and to appoint a special board of successor trustees, which may be the State Board of Trustees for that state, who shall thereupon automatically hold title to all property.

2. Furthermore, in the event of dissension within a local church of the Church of God, the state overseer of the Church of God for the state in which the local church is located shall have authority to declare the offices of the Local Board of Trustees vacant and to appoint a special Board of Trustees, which may be the State Board of Trustees, as successors to the Local Board of Trustees, and such special board so appointed shall automatically then hold title to the local property both real and personal.

3. If a sufficient number of qualified members are not available in any local church to constitute the Board of Trustees, another or others may be selected from another church.

4. Any person appointed to said Local Board of Trustees shall be a member in good standing of the Church of God. If at any time, any member of the said local board shall cease to be a member in good standing, or if by any reason, whether of death, removal, incapacity, or unwillingness to perform any duty of his office, or further, at the discretion of the state overseer, his place on the board may be declared vacant by the state overseer. The same authority that declares said office vacant is authorized to appoint another person to serve until the time for regular appointments, and the one so appointed shall have the same authority, responsibilities and duties as held by the one removed.

S57. INCORPORATION OF LOCAL CHURCHES [1994]

The Church of God is incorporated in the state of Tennessee as a 501 (C) (3) not-for-profit organization. There are certain occasions that require a local church to incorporate. It is understood that an incorporated local church does not lose its ecclesiastical relationship to the Church of God (Cleveland, Tennessee, U.S.A.) and the attributes of that relationship. The act of incorporation merely creates a legal entity to hold in trust the properties, both real and personal, of the Church of God (Cleveland, Tennessee, U.S.A.).

All churches that request to incorporate must first be approved in writing by the International Executive Committee. All charter/documents for incorporation of a local church must include the following clauses:

A. Providing a place of worship for its members, who shall be members in good standing of the Church of God, Cleveland, Tennessee, U.S.A., and conducting the affairs of the congregation according to the rules and regulations of the Church of God, Cleveland, Tennessee, U.S.A., and specifically the International General Assembly *Minutes* of the Church of God, Cleveland, Tennessee, U.S.A., promoting the cause of Christianity in accord with the teachings, tenets, and customs of the Church of God, Cleveland, Tennessee, U.S.A., receiving, managing, and disbursing gifts, bequests, and other funds for the benefit of the congregation and the Church of God, Cleveland, Tennessee, U.S.A., owning and maintaining suitable buildings and facilities necessary for their acquisition, upkeep, maintenance and sale, all in accord with the International General Assembly *Minutes* of the Church of God, Cleveland, Tennessee, U.S.A.

B. In the event this corporation shall cease to exist, or depart from the polity of the Church of God, Cleveland, Tennessee, U.S.A., as expressed in the International General Assembly *Minutes* of the Church of God, Cleveland, Tennessee, U.S.A., and otherwise, the assets of the corporation shall revert to the State Trustees for the Church of God in the state of _____, or to one or more organizations described in Section 501 (C) (3) of the Internal Revenue Code (U.S.A.) or the corresponding sections of any prior or future Internal Revenue Code (U.S.A.). Further, that the proceeds/assets from the disposition must go directly into real property purchases or improvements.

C. Once a charter for incorporation of a local church is filed with the state government, a copy of the approved charter is to be sent to the Church of God state office for the state in which the local church is situated.

S58. APPROVAL OF CONSTRUCTION, PURCHASE, OR REMODELING PLANS FOR LOCAL CHURCH [1994]

The state overseer shall require any local church in his state, before acquiring property, beginning or contracting for construction or purchase of a new church or educational building or a parsonage, or remodeling of such a building, if the cost will exceed 10 percent of its value, to submit for consideration and approval a statement of the need for the proposed facilities, preliminary architectural plans, and estimate of the cost, and a financial plan for defraying such costs. Before finally approving the building project, the state overseer or his designee shall ascertain whether the preliminary architectural design and financial programs have been reviewed, evaluated, and approved by proper authorities.

S59. ALL PROPERTY HELD FOR CHURCH OF GOD [1994]

All property, real or personal, held by or for a particular local church, state office, department or agency, whether legal title is lodged in a corporation, a trustee or trustees, or an unincorporated association, is held in trust nevertheless for the use and benefit of the Church of God, Cleveland, Tennessee, U.S.A.

The centralized governmental structure of the Church of God (Cleveland, Tennessee, U.S.A.) does not provide for local church ownership of properties outside the trust relationship for the sole and exclusive use and benefit of the Church of God (Cleveland, Tennessee, U.S.A.). All deed conveyances, or other actions purporting to effect ownership or control of real or personal property, which are inconsistent with the requirements as set forth in these International General Assembly *Minutes* are deemed invalid and ineffective to alter the essential trust relationship for the benefit of the Church of God (Cleveland, Tennessee, U.S.A.).

Where there does not exist an express trust covering real or personal properties utilized by local churches, then an implied trust in favor of the Church of God (Cleveland, Tennessee, U.S.A.) exists by virtue of the Church of God polity as expressed in these *Minutes*.

S60. AFFILIATION WITH CHURCH OF GOD [1994]

Non-Church of God churches that wish to affiliate with the Church of God will be allowed to join as associate churches. They shall be able to retain ownership of their properties. They shall make monthly reports to the state/regional and general offices with the same financial accountability as International General Assembly congregations. The pastor shall submit to a background check, and he/she shall secure Church of God ministerial credentials in accordance with the denomination's polity.

Further, appropriate forms of organization shall be processed in a legal business meeting to show acceptance of the faith, government, polity, and practices of the Church of God, and willingness to abide by the actions of the International General Assembly as it relates to their status as an associate church. In order to be accepted as an associate church, the group must accept the basic doctrinal commitments, teachings, and practical commitments as stated on pages 19-30 of this book of *Minutes, Church of God Book of Discipline, Church Order and Governance.*

An associate church can remove its associate status by placing the church properties on a Church of God warranty deed with the approval of the administrative bishop and the state/regional council (74th A., 2012).

S61. INVESTMENTS AND LOANS
(44th A., 1952, p. 34; 46th A., 1956, pp. 24, 25; 48th A., 1960, p. 32; 50th A., 1964, p. 61; 52nd A., 1968, pp. 50, 51; 62nd A., 1988, Journal, pp. 48, 49; [1996]).

MINISTERS' RETIREMENT PLANS

A. Investment and Loans

The Ministers' Retirement Plans (Aged Ministers' Plan and Church of God Ministers' Retirement Plan), in excess of a reasonable operating reserve, are to be invested at a fair market rate. Said investments are to be made by the Board of Trustees of the Church of God Benefits Board, Inc. upon recommendation by the Investment Committee.

B. Policy on Loans

The interest rate of local church loans from the Ministers' Retirement Plans (Aged Ministers' Plan and Church of God Ministers' Retirement Plan) is to be determined by the Board of Trustees of the Church of God Benefits Board, Inc. Amortization of loans is not to exceed twenty (20) years.

Loans from the Ministers' Retirement Plans (Aged Ministers' Plan and Church of God Ministers' Retirement Plan) are to be made according to the following criteria:
1. Certified appraisal
2. First mortgage required
3. Underwritten by State Council
4. Certified resolution by local church conference
5. Loss payee clause on insurance policy
6. Title insurance
7. Financial statement reflecting ability to repay
8. Loan not to exceed sixty percent (60%) of appraised value

The borrower shall be provided an amortization schedule covering the period of the loan. All delinquent payments received more than 10 days after the due date shall be charged a two percent (2%) late penalty. The two percent (2%) penalty for late payments shall be waived in the event payments must be made from state funds.

S62. CHURCH PROMOTION

I. EDUCATION PROGRAM

No church shall implement a Christian day school without permission from the state overseer. It is further suggested that pastors be advised that guidance can be furnished from the [General Board of Education and the State Board of Ministerial Development] (57th A., 1978, p. 38; 64th A., 1992, p. 78).

II. KNOW YOUR CHURCH WEEK

A week is to be set aside to be known as Know Your Church Week, and all legitimate efforts are to be concentrated to better inform our people of their own church, its doctrines, and the way it works. Concentration is to be on promotion of our church publications during this week (43rd A., 1950, p. 20; [1972]).

S63. WOMEN'S MINISTRIES (LOCAL CHURCH) [WOMEN'S DISCIPLESHIP] (31st A., 1936, pp. 32, 35; 45th A., 1954, p. 32; 53rd A., 1970, p. 43; 54th A., 1972, pp. 44, 45; 67th A., 1998, p. 52); [2014]

I. NAME

1. That each local church organize and maintain a ministry which shall be generally known as Church of God Women's Discipleship Ministries.

2. Where a ministry of this type is functioning under a different name, it may continue, if they so desire.

II. OFFICERS

The local church Women's Discipleship Committee shall consist of a president, vice president, and secretary-treasurer, of which the pastor is chairman. The manner of selecting, electing, or appointing these officers shall be left up to the pastor.

III. PRESIDENT

The president shall:

1. Preside at each meeting of the Women's Discipleship Ministries.

2. Be responsible for the general promotion of the Women's Discipleship Ministries in the local church.

3. Consult with the pastor about times and places of special services, such as in rest homes, prisons, and hospitals.

With the aid of the Women's Discipleship Ministries, consult with the pastor about worthy projects for the church.

IV. VICE PRESIDENT

The vice president shall:

1. Assist the president.

2. In the absence of the president, preside over regular meetings of the Women's Discipleship Ministries.

V. SECRETARY-TREASURER

The secretary-treasurer shall:

1. Keep a record of all regular meetings of the Women's Discipleship Ministries.

2. Keep a record of all finances and give a report of same to the Women's Discipleship Ministries at regular meetings.

3. Report each month to the state Women's Discipleship president, which will also include the YLM (Young Ladies Ministries) report.

4. Disburse monies when authorized to do so by the Women's Discipleship Ministries, the president, and with the approval of the pastor.

VI. Purposes and Objectives

Some of the purposes of the Women's Discipleship Ministries, under the guidance of the Women's Discipleship Committee and pastor, are to meet each week, or as often as convenient, to engage in prayer for the welfare of the church and the lost, to visit the sick, rest homes, prisons, PTAs, and other worthy civic organizations where their influence could be effective for God, the church, and the community. Further, they are to raise funds to be disbursed in behalf of the local church, state, and general work, after consulting with and having the approval of their pastor.

S64. SUNDAY SCHOOL (63rd A., 1990, pp. 76, 77)

The Sunday school represents the primary disciple-making agency in the local church. Its potential contribution to the lives of the people cannot be overestimated. Because of this, it deserves the best that can be provided in planning, organizing, coordinating, and supervising a quality program.

Therefore we recommend,

That each local church sponsor a Sunday school for the purpose of helping individuals grow in the knowledge and grace of God through regular and balanced study of the Scriptures.

That all Sunday schools function according to the guidelines established by the Ministry of Youth and Discipleship.

That each Sunday school be characterized by the following elements: (1) an environment of true Christian fellowship, (2) meaningful interaction with the Word of God, (3) a continual pointing of people toward worship and Christian service, and (4) a consistent outreach to the lost.

That each pastor be active in the promotion and execution of an aggressive Sunday school ministry.

That all Sunday school staff members be involved in the Church Training Course program on an ongoing basis.

That Sunday school outreach and extension attendance be reported according to the instructions given on the local church treasurer's report form.

That all Sunday schools use Church of God curricula, where practical.

That Sunday schools be established when new churches are set in order.

That Sunday schools be established as opportunities to organize new churches.

That the Sunday school in each new church be provided free literature by the Church of God Publishing House the first quarter following the organization of the church.

S65. FAMILY TRAINING HOUR AND/OR YPE
(63rd A., 1990, pp. 77, 78)

1. The acronym *YPE* (Young People's Endeavor) shall not be deleted from the book of **Minutes** of the International General Assembly, and that each time the term *Family Training Hour* is used in the **Minutes**, that "and/or YPE" be included.

2. The Church of God Family Training Hour and/or YPE is a midweek evangelistic and educational program sponsored by the local church to provide personalized, age-level training for each member of the family. The Family Training Hour and/or YPE sets forth a structure to provide each member of the family with a sense of belonging, to help develop talents, channel the desire to serve, promote spiritual growth, and train for Christian service.

Therefore, we recommend, that each local church establish a weekly Family Training Hour and/or YPE program designed to fulfill the following objectives: (1) motivate a sense of mission—both spiritual and secular—in each member of the family, (2) mobilize the family for New Testament service and worship, (3) magnify the importance of God's Word in family life, (4) maintain a fresh emphasis on the work of the Holy Spirit in directing family affairs, and (5) minister to family needs and relationships.

That each Family Training Hour and/or YPE function according to the guidelines established by the Ministry of Youth and Discipleship.

CHURCH GOVERNMENT— PERSONNEL
(S66 through S73)

(The rulings in this division of the *Book of Discipline, Church Order, and Governance* apply only to the United States of America.)

S66. EMPLOYMENT OF FAMILY MEMBERS
(44th A., 1952, p. 31)

The general officials and all other Ministry heads of the church shall refrain from employing members of their immediate family if said employees are to work under their personal supervision.

Where the state overseer receives the limit in salary and expenses, no member of his immediate family shall be employed as state secretary and treasurer.

S67. COMPENSATION FOR STATE LEADERS

I. STATE OVERSEER (64th A., 1992, pp. 88, 89)

A. Compensation

After a study has been made of the United States government cost-of-living index, the compensation of state overseers shall be set annually by the International Executive Council and become effective on September 1 of each year.

B. Other Compensation and Appropriations

1. One-half of the state overseer's Social Security tax (which is to be reported as taxable income according to the information of federal income tax consultants)

2. Contribution of an amount equal to a minimum of five percent of the state overseer's compensation to the Church of God Ministers' Retirement Plan for the state overseer

3. Premiums for medical insurance coverage

4. Reimbursement for expenses incurred in official business on the general level

5. The State Council is authorized to reimburse expenses incurred for official business on the state level, where funds are available.

6. The State Council is authorized to approve other gifts to the state overseer of up to $5,000 annually, directly from the state treasury.

II. STATE YOUTH AND DISCIPLESHIP DIRECTOR
(64th A., 1992, pp. 89, 90)

A. Compensation

After a study has been made of the United States Government cost-of-living index, the compensation of the state directors of Youth and Discipleship shall be set annually by the International Executive Council and become effective on September 1 of each year.

B. Other Compensation and Appropriations

1. One-half of the state director's Social Security tax (which is to be reported as taxable income according to the information of federal income tax consultants)

2. Contribution of an amount equal to five percent of the state director's compensation to the Church of God Ministers' Retirement Plan for the state director

3. Premiums for medical insurance coverage

4. Reimbursement for expenses incurred for official business on a general level

5. The State Council is authorized to reimburse expenses incurred in official business on the state level, where funds are available.

III. STATE EVANGELISM AND MISSIONS DIRECTOR
(64th A., 1992, pp. 89, 90)

A. Compensation

After a study has been made of the United States government cost-of-living index, the compensation of state directors of Evangelism and Missions shall be set annually by the Executive Council and become effective on September 1 of each year.

B. Other Compensation and Appropriations

1. One-half of the state director's Social Security tax (which is to be reported as taxable income according to the information of federal income tax consultants)

2. Contribution of an amount equal to five percent of the state director's compensation to the Church of God Ministers' Retirement Plan for the state director

3. Premiums for medical insurance coverage

4. Reimbursement for expenses incurred for official business on a general level

5. The State Council is authorized to reimburse expenses incurred in official business on the state level, where funds are available.

S68. COMPENSATION FOR PASTORS
(64th A., 1992, pp. 81-84; 71st A., 2006, pp. 44, 45; 77th A., 2018).

I. BASIC COMPENSATION
"Do ye not know that they which minister about holy things live of the things of the temple? and they which wait at the altar are partakers with the altar? Even so hath the Lord ordained that they which preach the gospel should live of the gospel" (1 Corinthians 9:13, 14).

The basic pastoral compensation shall consist of the following, based on the availability of appropriate tithe funds in the local church:

1. The compensation as designated for the appropriate membership category in **S69. PASTOR'S MINIMUM COMPENSATION SCALE**.

2. One-half of the pastor's Social Security tax (which is to be reported as taxable income according to the information of federal income tax consultants)

3. Premiums for health insurance coverage

4. Contribution by the local church to the Church of God Ministers' Retirement Plan for the pastor of an amount equal to at least ten percent of the cash compensation received by the pastor

5. Adequate housing accommodations, including utilities

These guidelines are ecclesiastical in application and are not a basis for any involvement outside the process of the Church of God.

II. UNDERPAID PASTORS
Pastors of churches where the tithe income is not sufficient to meet the Pastor's Minimum Compensation Scale shall receive 90 percent of the gross tithe. Further, that churches where the tithe income is not sufficient to pay the pastor's salary according to the minimum scale should endeavor to increase the pastor's income in an amount equal to minimum scale or more through freewill offerings or other means.

III. EXPENSES AND OTHER BENEFITS
There is clear instruction in the Scripture which admonishes the members of the church to recognize effective and fruitful spiritual leadership. *"Let the elders that rule well be counted worthy of double honour, especially they who labour in the word and doctrine. The labourer is worthy of his reward"* (1 Timothy 5:17, 18).

BOOK OF DISCIPLINE, CHURCH ORDER, AND GOVERNANCE 175

Therefore, all churches are encouraged to provide automobile travel expense allowances and to provide incentives such as higher percentages of retirement, annuity and insurance plans, and so forth, based on increases in finances, pastoral responsibility, pastoral effectiveness, and longevity.

The church to which the pastor has been appointed should pay reasonable moving expenses.

IV. SUPPLEMENTAL RETIREMENT BENEFIT PROGRAM

That we amend the 2008 book of *Minutes*, page 169, S70. Compensation for Pastors, VI. Supplemental Pastor's Retirement Fund, by deletion, and that the monies be used to fund the participants in the Aged Ministers Fund until such time as the fund liabilities cease, as determined by a certified actuarial report. Further, that a report on the status of the Aged Ministers Fund be given [to the International General Council] at each International General Assembly (73rd A., 2010, p. 188).

V. COST-OF-LIVING ADJUSTMENT (70th A., 2004 p. 56)

Annually, the International Executive Council shall make a study of the United States government's cost-of-living index. Afterwards, the Council shall authorize accordingly an adjustment in the **Pastor's Minimum Compensation Scale**, to become effective on September 1 of each year. Announcement of this annual adjustment shall be made by correspondence.

VI. COMPENSATION INCREASE

That the current **Pastor's Minimum Compensation Scale** be increased by 10 percent effective September 1, 2002 (69th A., 2002, p. 50).

S69. PASTOR'S MINIMUM COMPENSATION SCALE
Effective September 1, 2018
(Based on 2017 scale with an increase of 2.2% COL)

Membership	Weekly Compensation	Membership	Weekly Compensation
1-25	$838.00	76-100	$986.00
26-50	$889.00	101-125	$1,034.00
51-75	$939.00	126-150	$1,084.00

Membership	Weekly Compensation	Membership	Weekly Compensation
151-175	$1,133.00	828-850	$1,698.00
176-200	$1,186.00	851-875	$1,716.00
201-225	$1,200.00	876-900	$1,733.00
226-250	$1,224.00	901-925	$1,758.00
251-275	$1,242.00	926-950	$1,775.00
276-300	$1,263.00	951-975	$1,798.00
301-325	$1,281.00	976-1000	$1,812.00
326-350	$1,304.00	1001-1050	$1,855.00
351-375	$1,321.00	1051-1100	$1,891.00
376-400	$1,342.00	1101-1150	$1,931.00
401-425	$1,360.00	1151-1200	$1,977.00
426-450	$1,384.00	1201-1250	$2,011.00
451-475	$1,399.00	1251-1300	$2,051.00
476-500	$1,422.00	1301-1350	$2,093.00
501-525	$1,441.00	1351-1400	$2,129.00
526-550	$1,464.00	1401-1450	$2,169.00
551-575	$1,479.00	1451-1500	$2,212.00
576-600	$1,498.00	1501-1550	$2,246.00
601-625	$1,519.00	1551-1600	$2,290.00
626-650	$1,540.00	1601-1650	$2,326.00
651-675	$1,560.00	1651-1700	$2,365.00
676-700	$1,579.00	1701-1750	$2,407.00
701-725	$1,595.00	1751-1800	$2,446.00
726-750	$1,621.00	1801-1850	$2,487.00
751-775	$1,639.00	1851-1900	$2,523.00
776-800	$1,655.00	1901-1950	$2,565.00
801-825	$1,677.00	1951-2000	$2,604.00

Churches with more than 2,000 members should follow the process of $20.00 per week increase in minimum salary for each increase of 50 members in continuing this scale.

Presently established churches whose pastor's salary structure is adversely affected by this scale should maintain their pastor's present compensation (observing annual adjustments) until membership has increased to a higher compensation bracket.

VII. PASTORAL SABBATICAL

We recommend that lead pastors and, at the lead pastor's discretion, also staff pastors, take a sabbatical for purposes of personal spiritual renewal and marriage/family strengthening. That the recommended sabbatical be taken upon completion of five (5) consecutive years of pastoral ministry, and that sabbaticals continue throughout the pastor's ministry career at five (5) year intervals. The five (5) years of pastoral ministry shall not be limited to the tenure of the pastor in the present location where he/she is serving.

We also recommend that the pastor's sabbatical be thirty (30) days in length and include total cessation of ministry roles and responsibilities for the full sabbatical period. The time line of a sabbatical shall be planned in advance—the pastor working with the local church leadership and calendar, so necessary preparations can be made for continued ministry in the local church during the sabbatical.

The state/regional overseer and district overseer are to be informed in advance of the sabbatical, and provided with dates involved, and information concerning ministry/leadership roles in the local church where the pastor serves, during his/her sabbatical. The local church where the pastor serves shall continue full compensation to him/her during the sabbatical period (77th A., 2018).

S70. COMPENSATION FOR OTHER PERSONNEL
(50th A., 1964, p. 60; 51st A., 1966, p. 58; 54th A., 1972, p. 43; 55th A., 1974, p. 53; 56th A., 1976, p. 48; 62nd A., 1988, Journal, pp. 50, 51; [1994])

I. ASSISTANT PASTOR
Social Security

1. Local churches shall pay to the assistant pastor one-half of the amount owed by the assistant pastor for participation in the

Social Security program. (This measure is retroactive to include the year of 1968.)

2. The amount paid [to the assistant pastor for Social Security tax] is to be reported as taxable income according to the information of federal income tax consultants.

II. FULL-TIME EVANGELIST

A. Church of God Ministers' Retirement Plan

Where the tithe of tithes sent to the state treasurer is sufficient, the State Council shall be permitted to pay for [the full-time evangelist's] participation in the Church of God Ministers' Retirement Plan and, also, monthly premiums on hospitalization insurance.

B. Expenses

That the expenses for housing, utilities, travel, lodging, and food (actual expense if lodging and meals are not provided during appointments) be allowed [the full-time evangelist] as determined by the International Executive Council.

III. SUPPLEMENTAL INCOME FOR UNDERPAID PASTORS/EVANGELISTS (43rd A., 1950, p. 15; 45th A., 1954, pp. 29, 30; [1974])

After state office expenses have been paid, the State Council is authorized to use the surplus tithe of tithes from the state treasury to supplement the income of underpaid pastors and evangelists.

S71. MINISTERS' RETIREMENT PLAN CHURCH OF GOD BENEFITS BOARD, INC.
(59th A., 1982, p. 42; 60th A., 1984, pp. 45, 46; [1994])

I. HISTORY

In 1982, the Church of God International General Assembly approved the creation of the Church of God Ministers' Retirement Plan.

The International Executive Council constituted the board of trustees with the power and duty to correct errors made in the operation and administration of the plan; to delegate authority to any agent or agents; to carry out the duties of the board; and to decide all other matters relating to the plan not otherwise specifically assigned under the provisions of the plan.

The International General Assembly, as noted in **S4., II., Item 1** of the Supplement to the 1992 *Minutes* of the Church of God 64th

International General Assembly, authorized and directed that the International Executive Council "shall consider and act upon any and all matters pertaining to the general interest and welfare of the Church of God." After a review and study of present issues affecting the benefits program of the church, the general overseer with the counsel of the International Executive Council appointed the Committee on Separation of Pension Funds on January 25, 1993. The committee was composed of Floyd H. Lawhon, chairman, Raymond F. Culpepper, Raymond E. Crowley, O. Wayne Chambers, and Robert E. Fisher to study and address certain issues. Their assigned mission was "to do an impact study on the separation of the pension funds and report back to the next International Executive Council session."

II. Scope of the Study

The Committee on Separation of Pension Funds made diligent inquiry and study of historical and present issues affecting the benefits programs of the church. In addition, the committee studied the performance and administration of the plans, and the need for changes to strengthen the church's benefits programs for the better maintenance and retirement income security of the ministry. Those included must be United States citizens who are ministers, their dependents and beneficiaries, evangelists, missionaries, lay workers, and employees and their dependents who are engaged in the work of assisting the Church of God in performing its ministries and carrying out its supporting programs.

The committee addressed the operations, management, and administration of the church's benefits program, with primary attention devoted to the separation of pension funds through a corporate trust from general church funds.

III. Consultants and Recommendation

The committee engaged qualified consultants to investigate, report, and advise the church concerning certain facts and issues. Consultants included the following: Buddy E. Kimsey, CPA of the firm of Kersey, Arnett & Kirksey, Certified Public Accountants, Wedgewood Office, 4395 N. Ocoee, Cleveland, Tennessee, 37312; Mike Mudry, Fellow in the Society of Actuaries, Hay Huggins & Co., 229 South 18th Street, Rittenhouse Square, Philadelphia, Pennsylvania; Gary S. Nash, attorney, Akin, Gump, Strauss, Hauer & Feld, L.L.P., 1700 Pacific Avenue, Suite 4100, Dallas, Texas 75201; and Michael E. Callaway, attorney, 140 Ocoee St., NE, Cleveland, Tennessee 37364-1169.

Consultants provided an analysis of the possible impact on the overall financial statements of the church if the pension funds were completely separated from the church financial statements. Consultants provided the following recommendation:

It is imperative to separate the pension funds (especially those of the Ministers' Retirement Fund) from the overall church operating assets, both to provide adequate protection of the assets of the funds, and to provide better operating information through the financial statements of the church.

IV. WALL OF SEPARATION

The committee received many requests expressing a great desire and need to "build a wall" to protect the pension assets from the claims of creditors of the church. The study made diligent inquiries of other mainline religious denominations and churches as to their policies and practices concerning the carrying out of the fiduciary responsibilities, and for the protection of pension and benefit funds from the claims of church creditors. Reports were received of multimillion dollar settlements and judgments against major church bodies.

The appointed committee met numerous times during the years 1993-94 and reported their findings and submitted recommendations to the International Executive Council recognizing the litigious society and climate in which the Church of God seeks to carry out its mission and ministries. The Committee on Separation of Pension Funds met with the International Executive Committee on December 7, 1993, to seek their input and ideas on preliminary findings and recommendations being considered.

V. COMMITTEE REPORT

Following extensive study, the appointed committee submitted their findings and recommendations to the International Executive Council in January 1994, for action which would strengthen the retirement income security of the ministry and staffs of the Church of God, provide a firm foundation for growth, management, and administration of the church's benefits programs, and receive wide support from church constituents.

A. The Report included some of the following findings:

1. The church desires and intends to separate, safeguard and shield the funds dedicated and intended to provide retirement

income security and welfare benefits under the church's benefit plans from the claims of creditors of the church.

2. Serving as the 24-member board of trustees for the management and administration of the pension and benefits plan, the International Executive Council is hindered in time, experiential expertise, and continuity of management necessary for addressing the special and complex operational issues of the benefit plans.

3. The church needs to reengineer its benefit, management, and administration structure to meet the needs of a fast growing church and to lay a new foundation in order to "build the wall" that will both protect the benefits funds and provide an effective management system.

4. The creation of a controlled affiliate church benefits board affords the opportunities to call on persons gifted in administration, money management, leadership, and other qualities for service in the trusteeship areas of the benefits program.

B. The Report made the following recommendations:

1. That the International Executive Council approve the incorporation of a nonprofit, controlled affiliate, church benefits board with trust powers, as in the form of articles of incorporation, and this board shall be the trustee of the Ministers' Retirement Plan and such other plans as the International Executive Council may determine.

2. That the Executive Committee, as part of its duties and authority, shall timely appoint the trustees from the membership of our local churches to serve on the Board of Trustees of the Church of God (Cleveland, Tennessee, U.S.A.) Benefits Board, Inc., in accordance with its articles of incorporation and by-laws, taking care to appoint gifted lay leaders to at least four of the eight trustee positions.

VI. INTERNATIONAL EXECUTIVE COUNCIL ACTION

During the January 18-21, 1994, meeting of the Church of God International Executive Council, the final report from the Committee On Separation of Pension Funds was presented.

The International Executive Council serving as the trustees for the Ministers' Retirement Plan duly authorized the incorporation of the Church of God Benefits Board, Inc., and requested the International Executive Committee to proceed promptly to search for qualified and capable candidates for trustee service and identify the persons to be appointed as the members of the initial Board of

Trustees of the Church of God Benefits Board, Inc., consistent with the terms and classifications of the proposed articles of incorporation.

VII. BOARD OF TRUSTEES AND ELECTED OFFICERS

The members of the board of trustees are appointed by the Church of God International Executive Committee.

The president and chief executive officer, secretary, chairman, and vice chairman of the board are elected by the board of trustees.

The president and chief executive officer of the Church of God Benefits Board, Inc., directs the benefits programs of the Church of God.

VIII. PURPOSE

The purpose of the corporation is to act as the trustee of the plans and funds collected through the various retirement and benefits plans maintained by the corporation for ministers, missionaries, evangelists, employees, and other functionaries and their beneficiaries of the Church of God (Cleveland, Tennessee, U.S.A.) and such organizations controlled by or affiliated with the Church of God.

IX. PRINCIPAL FUNCTION

The corporation's principal function is the administration and funding of plans and programs for the provision of retirement benefits and welfare benefits for the ministers, missionaries, evangelists, employees, and other functionaries (and their widows, orphans or other beneficiaries) of the Church of God (Cleveland, Tennessee, U.S.A.) and such organizations controlled by or affiliated with the Church of God.

For more information, contact President/CEO, Church of God Benefits Board, Inc., P.O. Box 4608, Cleveland, TN 37320-4608. Phone: (423) 478-7131, or Fax: (423) 478-7889. *www.benefitsboard.com*

S72. AGED MINISTERS' PENSIONING PLAN

(41st A., 1946, pp. 27-29)

[Enrollments in the Aged Ministers' Pensioning Plan ceased as of December 31, 1982. Applications for benefits from this plan ceased as of August 31, 1992. As of that date, the contributions of eligible ministers enrolled in the plan, who had not as yet applied for a pension, were either (1) applied toward the purchase of a guaranteed annuity for the minister, or (2) rolled over into the Church of God Ministers' Retirement Plan in the name of

the minister. For a more detailed description of this plan, see the Supplement of the 1992 Minutes of the International General Assembly, S65.]

Based upon actuarial studies, the Aged Ministers' Pension Fund, Disabled Ministers' Pension Fund, and the Ministers Widows' Fund shall be adjusted by the International Executive Council according to the needs of the funds (74th A., 2012).

S73. INSURANCE

I. MINISTERIAL INSURANCE

Life Insurance-General

1. Any minister or member may carry insurance with any regular life insurance company.

2. Should anyone unite with the church who has insurance with a fraternal or secret order, he may continue his insurance with said order, provided he does not attend their secret meetings (35th A., 1940, pp. 31, 32).

Group Life

On August 30, 1928, the Church of God provided a group life insurance policy for its ministers.

Dividends

All dividends from the ministerial group insurance shall be paid to the general church treasury and credited to the general tithe fund (32nd A., 1937, p. 35; 35th A., 1940, p. 31; 46th A., 1958 p. 26).

II. PERSONNEL INSURANCE

Employees of the Church of God working in the various state offices shall be permitted to secure group life insurance, provided they pay the full premium at the prevailing rate (50th A., 1964, p. 66).

**BUSINESS SESSION
CHURCH OF GOD
77th INTERNATIONAL GENERAL ASSEMBLY**

Convening at the
Orange County Convention Center
Orlando, Florida
Friday, 1:30 to 4:00 p.m., August 3, 2018

CHURCH OF GOD
INTERNATIONAL EXECUTIVE COUNCIL

(The International Executive Committee,
with the Council of Eighteen,
comprise the International Executive Council of the Church of God.)

International Executive Committee

Nominated by the International General Council,
and Elected by the International General Assembly,
to Serve 2016-2020:

General Overseer	*Timothy Mark Hill*
First Assistant General Overseer	*Raymond F. Culpepper*
Second Assistant General Overseer	*J. David Stephens*
Third Assistant General Overseer	*David E. Ramírez S.*
Secretary General	*John D. Childers*

Council of Eighteen

Elected by the International General Council
to Serve 2018-2020:

Mark L. Williams	*Travis C. Johnson*
Gary J. Lewis	*Eliezer Bonilla*
H. Loran Livingston	*Thomas A. Madden*
Ishmael Prince Charles	*Niko Njotorahardjo*
Kevin M. McGlamery	*Barry A. Clardy*
Sean Stewart O'Neal	*Keith L. Ivester*
Gerald E. McGinnis	*Jerry D. Madden*
Timothy Wayne Oldfield	*T. Wayne Dority*
T. Bryan Cutshall	*Terry R. Hart*

*Ex Officio Members: moderator of
the Full Gospel Church of God in South Africa,
and the Overseer of the Church of God in Indonesia*

MINISTRY LEADERS

Nominated by the International General Council, and Elected by the International General Assembly, to serve 2016-2020:

Ministry of Youth and Discipleship

Director	David C. Blair
Assistant Director	Rob Bailey

Ministry of World Missions

Director	David M. Griffis
Assistant Director	M. Thomas Propes

RECOMMENDATIONS APPROVED, AND RESOLUTIONS ADOPTED, BY THE CHURCH OF GOD 77TH INTERNATIONAL GENERAL ASSEMBLY
(In Business Session, Friday, 1:30 to 4:00 p.m., August 3, 2018)

Note: references herein citing locations in the book of *Minutes—Church of God Book of Discipline, Church Order, and Governance,* are to the 2016 book of *Minutes.*

RECOMMENDATIONS

1. Resolution Regarding Visional Actualization

WHEREAS, we have been challenged with the vision to FINISH the Great Commission; and

WHEREAS, the accomplishment of this task will require the concerted effort and resources of the body of Christ; and

WHEREAS, this task will necessitate us to reimagine, retool, and revise methods, strategies, and programs to be effective, efficient, and relevant;

BE IT THEREFORE RESOLVED, that the general overseer, in consultation with the other members of the International Executive Committee, appoint a Task Force on Visional Actualization, that is representative of the church, including ministers and laity, men and women, and being ethnically diverse; and

BE IT FURTHER RESOLVED, that this Task Force specifically focus on the following areas, and prepare recommendations for the International Executive Council to consider for implementation and, as necessary, inclusion on the International General Council agenda for 2020:

A. Evaluation of the various ministries of the Church of God International Offices, to determine the value added to local churches; and to develop an instrument for state/regional offices to determine the value their programs and ministries are adding to the local church;

B. Assessment of the budget of the Church of God International Offices to determine the funding priorities supporting the core values of the church and finishing the Great Commission;

C. Review of the systems (including elections and appointments) and programs of the church, considering multinational and multigenerational cultures, including language-specific resources, cultural variants, and so forth;

D. Appraisal of church planting and church revitalization efforts and funding with a goal to enlarge and enhance the effectiveness of these priorities;

E. Analysis of the need for, and promotion of, ministerial recruitment, development, and placement in the Western USA, and other areas;

F. Refine, expand, and promote the current affiliation and amalgamation opportunities and procedures; and devise policy guidelines for multisite campuses; and

BE IT FINALLY RESOLVED, that a report of the work of this Task Force be prepared and made available to the 2020 International General Council.

2. **Actualization of a Global Context of Ministry**

   That we amend page 69, **S5. International Executive Council, III. Duties and Authorities,** by adding the following as **item 15:**

   15. The International Executive Council is tasked with the responsibility of actualizing a global context of ministry to include, but not limited to, enhancing the availability of language-specific resources; recognition and utilization of international leaders during general church events, refining programs, methods, and systems to reflect the international nature of the church; and challenging the church to think globally.

3. **Church Planting and Revitalization Task Force**

   That we amend page 132, **S39. EVANGELISM PROGRAM,** by inserting the following as the first paragraph:

   Each state/region establish a Church Planting and Revitalization Task Force and Training Center for the purpose of assessing, coaching, training, and sending church planters, as well as assisting senior pastors to revitalize and grow local congregations, thereby fulfilling the vision and commitment of the Church of God.

4. **Resolution Regarding Doctrinal Affirmation**

WHEREAS, the Church of God globally stands for the whole Bible rightly divided, and for the New Testament as the only rule of faith and practice; and

WHEREAS, the Church of God Declaration of Faith and Doctrinal Commitments remain the definitive statements of our beliefs; and

WHEREAS, we are living in a world that is constantly changing, and the calls to adapt our beliefs to prevailing societal norms or personal experiences are becoming more frequent;

BE IT THEREFORE RESOLVED, that we reaffirm our commitment to our core beliefs and values as stated in the latest edition of the book of *Minutes* of the Church of God International General Assembly—the *Church of God Book of Discipline, Church Order, and Governance;* and

BE IT FURTHER RESOLVED, that we communicate and emphasize the doctrinal distinctives of sanctification subsequent to the new birth, and baptism in the Holy Ghost subsequent to a clean heart; and

BE IT FURTHER RESOLVED, that we intentionally teach and proclaim our belief in the Pentecostal distinctive of speaking in other tongues as the initial evidence of the baptism in the Holy Spirit, and living a Spirit-empowered life; and

BE IT FURTHER RESOLVED, that our ministers prayerfully reaffirm their commitment to and belief in these doctrinal statements; and

BE IT FURTHER RESOLVED, that we continually seek to address current social issues in love, considering Biblical standards, not prevailing societal views; and

BE IT FURTHER RESOLVED, that to ensure generational continuity of faith, we instruct our youth in these doctrinal beliefs; and

BE IT FINALLY RESOLVED, that this resolution be placed in the book of *Minutes* following the **DOCTRINAL COMMITMENTS**.

5. Resolution Regarding Structural Acclimation

WHEREAS, while the Church of God has a structure with certain distinctives to our movement that has served us well throughout our history, at times it is necessary to refocus, retool, and recalibrate to accelerate our harvest goals; and

WHEREAS, the ministries of our movement have been supported by the tithing and giving of our faithful constituents; and

WHEREAS, throughout our history our ministers and churches have reported the progress of their ministry to their respective offices; and

WHEREAS, there is a need for elections and appointments to reflect the multicultural diversity of our movement; and

WHEREAS, enhanced preparation and effectiveness of state/regional leaders will provide more effective ministry and administrative success, so that focused appointments can provide for greater missional impact;

THEREFORE BE IT RESOLVED, that this 77th International General Council give attention to consistency in tithing and reporting by ministers and churches; and

BE IT FURTHER RESOLVED, that careful consideration be made of our voting and appointment processes to assure that they reflect our multicultural diversity and enhance our missional impact; and

BE IT FURTHER RESOLVED, that consideration be given to the state Youth and Discipleship director's length of tenure; and

BE IT FURTHER RESOLVED, that a Task Force be appointed to study considerations for greater global missional impact by the Church of God; and

BE IT FINALLY RESOLVED, that we consider the measures presented to this 77th International General Council for key and critical matters associated with structural acclimation with a sense of Kingdom urgency, so our movement can accelerate our harvest goals spiritually, missionally, and administratively in order to FINISH the Great Commission.

6. **International Executive Council and General Overseer Duties**

   A. That page 68, **S5. INTERNATIONAL EXECUTIVE COUNCIL, III. Duties and Authorities, Item 8,** be amended by striking the word *shall* and inserting the words *be authorized to*.

   So as to read:
   The general overseer, with the International Executive Council, be authorized to give one of his assistants the World Missions portfolio and assign his duties and authorities.

   B. That page 73, **S7. GENERAL OVERSEER, II. Duties and Authorities, Item 5,** be amended by inserting the words *be authorized to* before the word *give*.

   So as to read:
   Together with the International Executive Council, *be authorized to* give one of his assistants the World Missions portfolio and assign his duties and authorities.

7. **Tenure of State Youth and Discipleship Director**
   That page 132, **S37. STATE YOUTH AND DISCIPLESHIP DIRECTOR, I.** Selecion, Item 2 be amended by striking *eight* and inserting *four*.

   So as to read:

   The state Youth and Discipleship director's term of office shall be for two years with a maximum of four consecutive years in a respective non-mission state. [Effective 2020 General Assembly.]

8. **Election and Appointment Process Study Commission**
   That a Study Commission be appointed to review the election and appointment process, including reflection of multicultural diversity with recommendations to the International Executive Council for implementation of, and as necessary, inclusion on the 2020 International General Council agenda.

9. **Resolution Regarding Ministrial Activation**

   WHEREAS, ministers are called of God for "equipping of the saints for the work of ministry, for the edifying of the body of Christ" (Ephesians 4:12); and

   WHEREAS, the times demand that our ministers be prepared academically, emotionally, and professionally to adequately tend to the needs of our constituency and finish the Great Commission; and

   WHEREAS, the ministry is rewarding, yet extremely stressful because of attacks [antagonism to ministry] both from inside and outside the church; and

   WHEREAS, the church's health is dependent upon the health and well-being of the minister;

   BE IT THEREFORE RESOLVED, that the general overseer, in consultation with the International Executive Committee, appoint a Task Force on Ministerial Activation, that is representative of the church, to include ministers and laity, men and women, and being ethnically diverse; and

   BE IT FURTHER RESOLVED, that this Task Force specifically focus on the following areas, and prepare recommendations for the International Executive Council to consider for implementation or, as necessary, inclusion on the International General Council agenda for 2020:

A. Enhancement of the well-being of ministers, and the procedures for the rehabilitation and reinstatement of ministers;

B. Harmonization of standards relative to applicants for ministry, reflecting the international nature of the church; and

C. Enhancement of the credentialing process; and

BE IT FINALLY RESOLVED, that a report of the work of this Task Force be prepared and made available to the 2020 International General Council.

10. **General Requirements of Applicants for Ministry**

That we amend page 95, **S21. APPLICANTS FOR MINISTRY, IV. General Requirements of Applicants for Ministry,** by adding the following as **item 7:**

7. International Exceptions. The following exceptions to the established ministerial credentialing process apply only to countries outside the United States and Canada:

A. That the first two levels of credentials be issued by the field director's office, upon recommendation by the regional superintendent and national overseer, following appropriate screening and testing.

B. That the history and polity sections of the examination for the first two ranks of ministry be redesigned to include an overview of the history and polity of the Church of God internationally, and a more detailed review of the national church history and polity where the examination is administered.

C. The Ordained Bishop Examination will remain unchanged.

11. **Meaning and Usage of the Term *Bishop***

That open Ministry Forums be conducted globally to provide opportunity for deliberate and meaningful discussion, dialogue, questions/answers and time for spiritual insight regarding the importance and understanding of ministry ranks, qualifications, and women in leadership positions, with attention upon the meaning and usage of the title *Bishop*. Following the forums, appropriate motion(s) be formulated by the International

Executive Council specifically addressing these stated issues and brought to the 2020 International General Council.

12. **Tithing and Reporting Consistency**
That we amend page 124, **S32. STATE OVERSEER, I. Selection,** by adding the following as **item 3:**

3. Further, that all credentialed ministers be active in both tithing and attendance in a local Church of God congregation within the state/region in which the vote/evaluation is conducted.

13. **Lee/PTS Ministerial Scholarship**
That a study commission be formed for the purpose of exploring a possible scholarship fund for Lee University and Pentecostal Theological Seminary students who pledge to serve as pastors or church planters in the Western USA, and in other areas of the United States. That the findings be brought back to the International Executive Council for consideration and possible inclusion on the 2020 International General Council agenda.

14. **Ministerial Position Criminal Background Checks**
That we amend page 108, **S29. INSTRUCTIONS FOR MINISTERS, I. General Instructions for Ministers,** by adding the following as item 11:

11. Any person placed/appointed/hired for a ministry position in a local congregation of the Church of God should have a criminal background check.

15. **Pastoral Placement**
That a Study Commission on Pastoral Placement be appointed to review the process and procedures of pastoral appointments and evaluation with recommendations presented to the International Executive Council for implementation or, as necessary, inclusion on the 2020 International General Council agenda.

16. **Pastoral Sabbatical**
That we amend page 173, **S68, COMPENSATION FOR PASTORS,** by adding the following as **VII. Pastoral Sabbatical:**

So as to read:
VII. Pastoral Sabbatical
We recommend that lead pastors and, at the lead pastor's discretion, also staff pastors, take a sabbatical for purposes of personal

spiritual renewal and marriage/family strengthening. That the recommended sabbatical be taken upon completion of five (5) consecutive years of pastoral ministry, and that sabbaticals continue throughout the pastor's ministry career at five (5) year intervals. The five (5) years of pastoral ministry shall not be limited to the tenure of the pastor in the present location where he/she is serving.

We also recommend that the pastor's sabbatical be thirty (30) days in length and include total cessation of ministry roles and responsibilities for the full sabbatical period. The time line of a sabbatical shall be planned in advance—the pastor working with the local church leadership and calendar, so necessary preparations can be made for continued ministry in the local church during the sabbatical.

The state/regional overseer and district overseer are to be informed in advance of the sabbatical, and provided with dates involved, and information concerning ministry/leadership roles in the local church where the pastor serves, during his/her sabbatical. The local church where the pastor serves shall continue full compensation to him/her during the sabbatical period.

17. **State Overseer Qualifications**
We recommend that page 124, **S32, STATE OVERSEERS, III. Qualifications**—be amended by adding the following as **item 6:**

6. The state overseer shall have served as the senior/lead pastor of a local church congregation for a minimum of five (5) years, or after having been elected to an International Office or Position in the Church of God. (Anyone under appointment as an Administrative Bishop, or as a Youth and Discipleship director, as of the 2018 General Assembly, shall be exempt from this item.)

18. **State Overseer Qualifications—Leadership Development**
That page 125, **S32, STATE OVERSEERS,** be amended by inserting the following as **VI. Continuing Leadership Development.**

VI. Continuing Leadership Development
State overseers shall actively participate in continuing leadership development and training courses as planned, directed, and implemented by the International Executive Committee.

19. District Overseers

That we amend page 134, **S43, DISTRICT OVERSEERS, II. Duties and Authorities,** by adding the following as **items 6 and 7:**

6. Annually, each district shall identify and participate in a church revitalization project within the district (where feasible).

7. Each district shall be encouraged to establish a goal for church planting every two years in partnership with the state office.

20. Exhorter

That we amend page 103, **S24, EXHORTER, II. Rights and Authorities, 4,** by deleting the words *In cases of emergency.*

So as to read:

The exhorter may be authorized by the state overseer to baptize converts and receive believers into fellowship of church membership (47th A., 1958, pp. 28, 29).

21. That we delete on page 103, **S24. EXHORTER, II. Rights and Authorities, item 6.**

6. Exhorters who are serving as helpers and assistants may receive tithes when available (21st A., 1926, p. 32). (This item deleted.)

22. Resolution Regarding Generational Assimilation

WHEREAS, the ministry pool of the Church of God has continued to age in the past few decades; and

WHEREAS, these aging ministers have contributed greatly to the establishment and advancement of the ministries of the Church of God; and

WHEREAS, a Caleb Generation of ministers has much to offer a new generation of God-called, Spirit-filled ministers by mentoring, advising, and guiding the younger generation; and

WHEREAS, a new generation of young ministers—the Jeremiah Generation—stands ready to march into the harvest with a decided determination to FINISH the Great Commission in their generation; and

WHEREAS, the Church of God must provide opportunities for upward mobility of potential leaders at all levels of ministry and administration; and

WHEREAS, there is an expressed need for assimilation of the generations into a dynamic, Spirit-empowered force to go into the harvest and FINISH the Great Commission; and

WHEREAS, a need exists for greater cooperation in ministry by both older and younger generations, so that we may complete the task assigned to us by our Lord in His Great Commission to the Church in Matthew 28:19-20;

THEREFORE, BE IT RESOLVED, that the International Executive Council of the Church of God implement ways and means to provide meaningful recognition and affirmation of aging ministers; and

BE IT FURTHER RESOLVED, that we embrace the Jeremiah Generation of emerging ministers in meaningful ways that will mobilize this army of younger ministers; and

BE IT FINALLY RESOLVED, that we consider practical actions for the assimilation of generations into a viable spiritual force for the work of the ministry and for the advancement of the Gospel, so the Church of God may FINISH the Great Commission.

23. **Ministry Life Planning**
That page 127, **S32, STATE OVERSEERS, VI. Duties and Authorities, 22,** be added so as to read:

22. That each state/regional office conduct an annual Ministry Life Planning Training event covering the issues and challenges of retirement planning, ministerial retirement transition, ministerial taxes, healthcare, and whole life health, assisting ministers of every age to approach the stages of life successfully, and to embrace the aging of ministry.

24. **Engaging the "Jeremiah Generation"**
That we amend page 127, **S32, STATE OVERSEERS, VI. Duties and Authorities,** by adding the following as 23:

23. That each State/Regional Overseer, in cooperation with the State/Regional Youth and Discipleship Director, lead pastors, student pastors, and the state/regional Ministerial Development Board (CAMS and MIP), adopt an annual plan for identifying,

mentoring/training, and engaging young men and women, designated as the "Jeremiah Generation," in both the local and state/regional ministry of the Church of God.

25. Generational Task Force

That a Generational Task Force be established to identify and embrace the differing requirements of generational ministry. The Generational Task Force will be appointed by the International Executive Committee and will meet at least yearly to provide input to the International Executive Committee regarding the needs of the various generations.

26. Aging of Ministry Task Force

That a Task Force be appointed to study the aging of ministry in the Church of God, and to find ways and means to provide meaningful recognition and affirmation of aging ministers, with recommendations to the International Executive Council for implementation of, or as necessary, inclusion on, the 2020 International General Council agenda.

27. Resolution Regarding Spiritual Acceleration

WHEREAS, from our humble beginning, we have been a movement characterized by our insistence upon the authority of God's Word; and

WHEREAS, our firm stand on Scriptural authority has led us to our fundamental statement that we accept the whole Bible, rightly divided, and the New Testament as our only rule for discipline and government; and

WHEREAS, we, as a movement, have delineated our basic beliefs in the document known as the Church of God Declaration of Faith; and

WHEREAS, we, as with other religious organizations, now face great and complex challenges to our historic faith; and,

WHEREAS, the Church of God sees itself as a divine work of the Holy Spirit, a vital part of a spiritual movement called to help usher in revival and bring renewal to a spiritually hungry world; and

WHEREAS, we have pledged our movement to FINISH, in this generation, the Great Commission given to the Church by our Lord in Matthew 28:19-20;

THEREFORE, BE IT RESOLVED, that this 77th International General Council of the Church of God diligently seeks to implement ways and means to foster renewed dedication and commitment to the core values of the Church of God as outlined in the *Minutes* of the International General Assembly; and

BE IT FINALLY RESOLVED that we consider appointing a Task Force to study and review the "Commitments to the Core Values of the Church of God," so that we may retain our unique position as one of the leading Pentecostal churches in the world.

28. **Core Values—Commitments to Our Mission and Vision**
That a Task Force be appointed to study ways to renew our commitment to our Mission and Vision Statement, with recommendations to the International Executive Council for implementation or, if necessary, inclusion on, the 2020 International General Council agenda.

MOTIONS FROM THE MOTIONS COMMITTEE:

29. To amend page 66: **S5 INTERNATIONAL EXECUTIVE COUNCIL, I. SELECTION,** by deleting paragraph 2 which currently reads:

The International Executive Council is comprised of the International Executive Committee and eighteen (18) elected members. Not less than nine (9) members shall be pastors at the time of their election. Further, two (2) members of the Council of Eighteen shall be at the time of their election foreign nationals residing and ministering outside the United States. No member of the International Executive Committee who has just completed his tenure of office shall be eligible to serve on the International Executive Council for the ensuing International General Assembly term.

And replacing it with:

The International Executive Council is comprised of the International Executive Committee and eighteen (18) elected members. Not less than twelve (12) members shall be pastors at the time of their election. Further, three (3) members of the Council of Eighteen shall be at the time of their election foreign nationals residing and ministering outside the United States. No member of the International Executive Committee who has just completed his tenure of office shall be eligible to serve on the International Executive Council for the ensuing International General Assembly term.

30. To amend page 172: **S68 COMPENSATION FOR PASTORS, I. BASIC COMPENSATION,** by amending paragraph 4 which currently reads:

Contribution by the local church to the Church of God Ministers' Retirement Plan for the pastor of an amount equal to at least five percent of the cash compensation received by the pastor.

And replace with:

Contribution by the local church to the Church of God Ministers' Retirement Plan for the pastor of an amount equal to at least ten percent of the cash compensation received by the pastor.

31. That we amend the *Minutes* on page 153, **S54. Financial System, Section III,** by adding the following paragraph:

5. Further, any pastor who is found at fault by an investigation committee, who has failed to send in his/her respective church reports for four (4) months or more, shall be subject to disciplinary action from his/her respective Administrative Bishop, up to revocation of credentials. The Administrative Bishop can make exceptions to this ruling on a case-by-case basis, and as is in compliance with the *Minutes* of the General Assembly, **S7. Section II, Paragraph 11,** under **Duties of the General Overseer.** The action of the Administrative Bishop must be approved by the general overseer of the Church of God (the Presiding Bishop) for final determination.

32. That we amend the *Minutes* on page 106, **S28. MINISTERIAL REPORTING, Section III,** replacing paragraph two with the following:

2. Further, he/she shall be notified in writing, that if he/she fails to report for a period of four (4) months, his/her credentials will be subject to revocation, after due disciplinary process on a case-by-case basis.

33. That we create a task force to study the reorganization of the Ministry of Youth and Discipleship, and the possibility of a partnership of this Ministry with Lee University and the Pentecostal Theological Seminary, to develop kids' and students' study series for use in kids' church and students' worship.

RESOLUTIONS:

Resolution of Appreciation to Presiding Bishop Timothy M. Hill

WHEREAS, Dr. Timothy M. Hill has faithfully served the Church of God during his lifetime as a dynamic Christian musician and songwriter, Pastor, Evangelist, State Youth Director, State Administrative Bishop, and Member of the International Executive Council; and

WHEREAS, he has provided executive leadership as Director of World Missions, wherein he expanded the global mission of the Church of God and its continuing benevolent global ministry through programs such as "Marcelly's Dream;" and

WHEREAS, his service as a member of the International Executive Committee for ten years has been distinguished by His passion for the Church of God and its role in the Kingdom of God; and

WHEREAS, as Presiding Bishop since 2016, his dedicated efforts to lead the Church of God to engage finishing the Great Commission through the FINISH COMMITMENT emphasis is reigniting a Spirit-filled passion to win the lost for Christ in this generation; and

WHEREAS, as Presiding Bishop since 2016, he has maintained an unprecedented awareness to raise up a younger generation of leaders, known as the "JEREMIAH GENERATION" that will lead the Church of God for decades to come; and

WHEREAS, he has focused all his efforts, leadership skills, and broad experience for furthering the Kingdom of God through the ministries of the Church of God tirelessly;

NOW THEREFORE BE IT RESOLVED, that we commit ourselves to fulfilling the Biblical mandates and mission of the Church in finishing the Great Commission; and

BE IT FURTHER RESOLVED, that we pray for God's continued empowerment of the ministries of the church, and for blessings upon Presiding Bishop Timothy M. Hill and his family for the ensuing years as he leads the Church of God.

Resolution of Appreciation to the Church of God International Executive Committee

WHEREAS, Presiding Bishop, Dr. Timothy M. Hill; First Assistant, Dr. Raymond F. Culpepper; Second Assistant, Dr. J. David Stephens; Third Assistant, Dr. David E. Ramirez S; and Secretary General, Dr. John D. Childers; have served the Church of God with distinction, humility, and integrity; and

WHEREAS, they have exemplified and demonstrated Biblical unity, the power of Christian teamwork, effective ministry acumen, financial accountability, and transparency in all aspects of denominational oversight through the "Let's Talk About It" series; and

WHEREAS, they have utilized all available media prowess to cast a vision for a Global Harvest, and have aggressively led the Church of God to follow a Global blueprint to FINISH the Great Commission in our lifetime; and

WHEREAS, the FINISH commitment engages the Church of God to FIND the lost and disenfranchised, INTERCEDE through prayer and worship, NETWORK servant leaders of all generations, INVEST our resources for greater effectiveness, SEND disciples to all nations, and reap a great Kingdom HARVEST; and

WHEREAS, they have reaffirmed the mission of the Church of God by further clarifying the Essential Alignment of Priorities, Paradigms and Purpose, Doctrinal Affirmation, and Visual Actualization; and

WHEREAS, they have initiated the JEREMIAH PROJECT, enabling the Church of God to provide a platform to identify, equip, release, empower, and highlight a generation of young leaders to lead today and into the future; and

WHEREAS, they have both called and led the Church of God to engage in a continual and consistent season of prayer and fasting; and furthermore, they have provided opportunity for the International Church to participate with them in seasons of prayer and fasting through social media; and

WHEREAS, they have provided the leadership to effectively establish a Church Planting Bank, and have reignited a fire of passion to plant new life-giving churches in the United States and around the world; and

WHEREAS, they have provided the leadership to effectively launch a Church Revitalization emphasis that provides the impetus for an established church to look at their past, examine their present, and cast new vision for their future; and

WHEREAS, they have provided leadership to train and release Church Planting Coaches, and Church Revitalization Coaches, to assist planters and pastors in their mission;

NOW THEREFORE BE IT RESOLVED, that the Church of God expresses its most profound gratitude and appreciation to the Church of God International Executive Committee for their leadership and partnership.

Resolution of Appreciation to the Church of God International Executive Council

WHEREAS, the 2016 Church of God International General Assembly elected into office (to serve 2016-2020) the general overseer, his assistants and the secretary general, which constitute the Church of God International Executive Committee; and

WHEREAS, eighteen councilors were elected (to serve 2016-2018) by the International General Council, duly ascribed to by the International General Assembly as the Council of Eighteen, to serve the Church of God in matters of governance, polity, and doctrine; and

WHEREAS, the International Executive Committee, with the Council of Eighteen, constitute the International Executive Council, which is duly authorized by the International General Assembly to meet together for the purpose of considering and acting upon all matters pertaining to the general interest and welfare of the Church of God; and

WHEREAS, members of the Church of God present matters pertaining to the general interest and welfare of the church to be considered as agenda items at this General Assembly; and

WHEREAS, at various times as set by the general overseer, the International Executive Council convened, prayed, reviewed, and deliberated on such matters, following the leading of the Holy Spirit, adopting recommendations and setting them forth as agenda items for this General Assembly; and

WHEREAS, these items were presented before the International General Council, and before this General Assembly, as the agenda to be discussed, amended, or modified as needed. That after much spirited deliberations, certain agenda items were adopted according to our polity and standards for the purpose of advancing the Kingdom of God and the mission of the global church;

NOW THEREFORE BE IT RESOLVED, that we, the International General Council, express our most sincere appreciation to every member of the International Executive Council for their leadership and commitment to serve. And further, we appreciate the many hours they have sacrificed away from their families, churches, and offices in preparation of the General Assembly agenda;

AND FINALLY, we appreciate the passion and humility demonstrated by the International Executive Council, as they worked faithfully, seeking the will of God for the future welfare of the Church of God.

Resolution of Appreciation to
The 77th International General Assembly Cabinet

WHEREAS, the first General Assembly of the Church of God in 1906 was sponsored, organized, and managed by the twenty-one delegates in attendance; and

WHEREAS, several of the 1906 Assembly delegates could be described as the precursors to the current International General Assembly Cabinet; and

WHEREAS, the 2018 International General Assembly Cabinet has had the immense logistical and organizational responsibility that required the involvement of numerous committees, hundreds of planners, designers, schedulers, professionals, specialists, workers, and auxiliary personnel; and

WHEREAS, the 2018 International General Assembly Cabinet devoted hundreds of hours of administration, preparation, and supervision that have resulted in a successful and enjoyable convention; and

WHEREAS, the appointed committees and personnel performed their duties in a proficient and professional manner;

NOW THEREFORE BE IT RESOLVED, that the 2018 International General Assembly leaders and delegates, express sincere and heartfelt appreciation to the 2018 General Assembly Cabinet, namely; Presiding Bishop Timothy M. Hill, Executive Bishop John D. Childers (Chairman), David Ray, Art Rhodes, David Blair, Dusty Wilson, Kenneth Bell, Kevin Brooks, Raymond Hodge, Anthony Pelt, Yvette Santana, and Dennis Watkins (Consultant) for their dedicated participation that ensured the fruitful, well-organized, and effective functioning of the 2018 International General Assembly of the Church of God.

Resolution of Appreciation to the City of Orlando, Florida

WHEREAS, the delegates of this 77th Church of God International General Assembly are indebted to our host city, Orlando, Florida, for a most successful meeting, July 31 through August 3, 2018; and

WHEREAS, the City of Orlando, Florida, along with its Mayor Buddy Dyer, and Visit Orlando, the official source for Orlando meetings and conventions, have welcomed the delegates of the Assembly, and have crafted meeting arrangements in a superior manner; and

WHEREAS, the City of Orlando, Florida has lived up to its nickname, "The City Beautiful," and has provided approximately 450 hotels and resorts for Assembly delegates, and has offered a variety of restaurants and world-class amusement parks for the Church of God Family; and

WHEREAS, the City of Orlando, Florida has offered easy accessibility to delegates via the airlines and interstate highways, and has offered one of America's largest convention centers in the Orange County Convention Center; and

WHEREAS, Orlando's Orange County Convention Center has spacious and comfortable meeting and exhibition areas, providing a pleasant and cordial environment for the Assembly; and

WHEREAS, the leadership, staff, volunteers, and citizens of the City of Orlando, Florida have once again gone beyond the call of duty to host this 77th Church of God International General Assembly;

NOW THEREFORE BE IT RESOLVED, that the International General Assembly leaders and delegates express their sincere and heartfelt appreciation to the City of Orlando, Florida, and to the Orange County Convention Center, for your hospitality shown to the delegates of this 77th International General Assembly, and we pray for God's continued blessings upon this city.

Resolution in Regard to
Unity in Finishing the Great Commission

WHEREAS, Jesus prayed for the unity of His followers: "That they all may be one" (John 17:21); and

WHEREAS, Jesus' prayer was answered prior to Pentecost, and on the Day of Pentecost (Acts 1:14; 2:1); and

WHEREAS, the apostle Paul called for the Church to endeavor to remain in unity (Ephesians 4:1-3); and

WHEREAS, the Church of God has accepted the FINISH Commitment to fulfill the Great Commission; and

WHEREAS, the accomplishment of this task will require that we partner together with one another in the Church of God, and that we partner with others in the body of Christ, realizing that together we can do more; and

WHEREAS, the body of Christ in 2018 has been made aware of the Finish 2030 Movement, a global church network of more than 2,400 Christian denominations encompassing nearly six hundred thousand churches, with the goal of doubling the size of the Church, and making it less likely for people to live on this earth and not hear the gospel of Jesus Christ; and

WHEREAS, the Early Church has given us the pattern of synergy in Acts 2, stated in the use of terms such as *they, together,* and *in common,* with the synergy among those early believers climaxing in their having "turned their world upside down;"

BE IT THEREFORE RESOLVED, that the Church of God makes unity, not just a stated value, but an actual practice, as we network, partner, and cooperate with other Evangelical and Pentecostal denominations in a Kingdom mind set to fulfill and finish the Great Commission, trusting that with God's help and favor, this will be accomplished.

Resolution in Regard to School Violence

WHEREAS, it appears to us that contemporary culture has become marked by violence, and this has been exhibited particularly against the most vulnerable in our societies; and

WHEREAS, we observe in the United States of America, that a culture of violence appears to have emerged among our school-aged children, and among our college students, demonstrated in the escalation of reported incidents of bullying and assault, and in the most extreme cases, the occurrence of horrific tragic events where multiple lives of our students have been lost as a result of violence; and

WHEREAS, violence in our schools at any level disrupts the educational environment, whether it occurs on campus, during transit to or from school, during school-sponsored events at any school level, or in communications through social media; and

WHEREAS, students who are the objects of any form of violence in their schools may experience trauma, fear, and anxiety that can significantly impact their lives; and

WHEREAS, we observe that many students and teachers have exemplified courage in the appropriate witness of their faith and manner of life in Christ, at the risk of experiencing violence in their schools; and

WHEREAS, Holy Scripture teaches that our children and youth are blessings from the Lord (Psalm 127:3), and directs us to provide for their training and development (Deuteronomy 6:6-7; Proverbs 22:6; Ephesians 6:4);

THEREFORE BE IT RESOLVED, that the Church of God extend prayers and compassion to all those students and families who have been touched by school violence, and for our schools, with the goal of obtaining peace and civility; and

BE IT BE FURTHER RESOLVED, that we encourage our ministers and laity to engage school and civic leadership to address school violence, to provide safe educational environments, and to encourage a culture of those long-held traits of good citizenship: love, respect, and accountability; and

BE IT FURTHER RESOLVED, that we commit our efforts to teach our students the traits of love, respect, and accountability as part of the proper behavior of Christian believers; and that we give diligent effort to support families and parents in our ministries where these traits can be reinforced; and

BE IT FINALLY RESOLVED, that we commend those students and teachers who have faithfully demonstrated their Christian faith and values in their daily lives in the face of school violence, and commit ourselves to prayers for divine protection and strengthening for them.

FINANCIAL REPORT
(Fiscal Years 2016-17 and 2017-18)

NOTICE

The Church of God Benefits Board
is not included in this Financial Report
because the finances of the Benefits Board
are kept entirely separate from the general funds of the Church of God.

The Church of God Benefits Board
operates for the benefit of Church of God ministers and employees,
but by federal law is required to exist and operate as an enterprise
distinctly separate from the Church of God.

For information about the Church of God Benefits Board,
contact the Benefits Board at:

Church of God Benefits Board

4205 North Ocoee Street

Cleveland, TN 37312

Telephone: (423) 478-7131

www.benefitsboard.com

FINANCIAL REPORT FOR THE YEAR 2016-2017

TITHE FUND
Balance on Deposit August 31, 2016 .... $		—
Receipts From the Field .... $		19,595,554
Less Appropriations--		
Aged Ministers .... $	1,265,074	
Disabled Ministers .... $	130,361	
IEC General Fund.................. $	1,278,833	
Ministers Widows.................. $	129,606	
Total Appropriations .... $	2,803,874	
Net Receipts from the Field .... $		16,791,680
Other Income .... $	1,264,893	
Total Net Receipts .... $		18,056,573
Disbursements .... $		17,918,568
Net Change - Assets/Liabilities...................... $		(138,005)
Balance on Deposit August 31, 2017................... $		0

AGED MINISTERS FUND
Balance on Deposit August 31, 2016................... $	1,724,641
Receipts... $	1,963,681
Disbursements .... $	2,358,267
Net Change - Assets/Liabilities...................... $	(808,813)
Balance on Deposit August 31, 2017................... $	521,242

BENEVOLENCES FUND
Balance on Deposit August 31, 2016................... $	83,204
Receipts... $	893
Disbursements .... $	—
Net Change - Assets/Liabilities...................... $	(893)
Balance on Deposit August 31, 2017................... $	83,204

BUILDING LOAN FUND
Balance on Deposit August 31, 2016................... $	2,198
Receipts... $	—
Disbursements .... $	—
Net Change - Assets/Liabilities...................... $	—
Balance on Deposit August 31, 2017................... $	2,198

CHURCH PLANTING
Balance on Deposit August 31, 2016................... $	—
Receipts... $	472,875
Disbursements .... $	120,679
Net Change - Assets/Liabilities...................... $	(110,537)
Balance on Deposit August 31, 2017................... $	241,658

CMT FUND 61
Balance on Deposit August 31, 2016 . . . . $ 159,820
Receipts . . . . $ 264,336
Disbursements . . . . $ 384,755
Net Change - Assets/Liabilities. . . . . $ (1,038)
Balance on Deposit August 31, 2017 . . . . $ 38,363

CMT FUND 62
Balance on Deposit August 31, 2016 . . . . $ 68,784
Receipts . . . . $ 239,182
Disbursements . . . . $ 263,151
Net Change - Assets/Liabilities. . . . . $ —
Balance on Deposit August 31, 2017 . . . . $ 44,816

CMT FUND 63
Balance on Deposit August 31, 2016 . . . . $ 120,700
Receipts . . . . $ 221,687
Disbursements . . . . $ 282,800
Net Change - Assets/Liabilities. . . . . $ —
Balance on Deposit August 31, 2017 . . . . $ 59,587

CMT FUND 64
Balance on Deposit August 31, 2016 . . . . $ 162,305
Receipts . . . . $ 248,187
Disbursements . . . . $ 383,583
Net Change - Assets/Liabilities. . . . . $ —
Balance on Deposit August 31, 2017 . . . . $ 26,908

CMT - ESCROW
Balance on Deposit August 31, 2016 . . . . $ 21,757
Receipts . . . . $ 220,409
Disbursements . . . . $ 229,792
Net Change - Assets/Liabilities. . . . . $ —
Balance on Deposit August 31, 2017 . . . . $ 12,374

COMMUNICATIONS FUND
Balance on Deposit August 31, 2016 . . . . $ 5,432
Receipts . . . . $ 827,979
Disbursements . . . . $ 830,891
Net Change - Assets/Liabilities. . . . . $ 726
Balance on Deposit August 31, 2017 . . . . $ 3,246

COMPUTER SERVICES
Balance on Deposit August 31, 2016 . . . . $ 251
Receipts . . . . $ 380,329
Disbursements . . . . $ 359,601
Net Change - Assets/Liabilities. . . . . $ (18,000)
Balance on Deposit August 31, 2017 . . . . $ 2,979

DISABLED MINISTERS FUND
  Balance on Deposit August 31, 2016 . . . . $ 156,804
  Receipts . . . . $ 130,361
  Disbursements . . . . $ 285,127
  Net Change - Assets/Liabilities. . . . . $ (1)
  Balance on Deposit August 31, 2017 . . . . $ 2,037

DISASTER RELIEF FUND
  Balance on Deposit August 31, 2016 . . . . $ 297,276
  Receipts . . . . $ 424,258
  Disbursements . . . . $ 636,559
  Net Change - Assets/Liabilities. . . . . $ —
  Balance on Deposit August 31, 2017 . . . . $ 84,975

DIVISION OF CARE
  Balance on Deposit August 31, 2016 . . . . $ 1,327,293
  Receipts . . . . $ 3,827,573
  Disbursements . . . . $ 3,413,815
  Net Change - Assets/Liabilities. . . . . $ (31,513)
  Balance on Deposit August 31, 2017 . . . . $ 1,709,538

DIVISION OF DISCIPLESHIP
  Balance on Deposit August 31, 2016 . . . . $ (585,169)
  Receipts . . . . $ 5,228,046
  Disbursements . . . . $ 5,399,916
  Net Change - Assets/Liabilities. . . . . $ 1,006,056
  Balance on Deposit August 31, 2017 . . . . $ 249,017

DIVISION OF EDUCATION
  Balance on Deposit August 31, 2016 . . . . $ 202,423
  Receipts . . . . $ 6,094,657
  Disbursements . . . . $ 5,416,031
  Net Change - Assets/Liabilities. . . . . $ 4,878
  Balance on Deposit August 31, 2017 . . . . $ 885,927

DIVISION OF WORLD EVANGELIZATION
  Balance on Deposit August 31, 2016 . . . . $ 319,036
  Receipts . . . . $ 3,250,969
  Disbursements . . . . $ 3,576,773
  Net Change - Assets/Liabilities. . . . . $ 4,698
  Balance on Deposit August 31, 2017 . . . . $ (2,070)

GENERAL ASSEMBLY
  Balance on Deposit August 31, 2016 . . . . $ (1,075,428)
  Receipts . . . . $ 1,202,810
  Disbursements . . . . $ 1,243,269
  Net Change - Assets/Liabilities. . . . . $ 622,193
  Balance on Deposit August 31, 2017 . . . . $ (493,694)

HELPING HANDS
Balance on Deposit August 31, 2016 .... $	1,774
Receipts .... $	139,508
Disbursements .... $	183,825
Net Change - Assets/Liabilities .... $	60,942
Balance on Deposit August 31, 2017 .... $	18,399

INSURANCE FUND
Balance on Deposit August 31, 2016 .... $	223,530
Receipts .... $	4,331,785
Disbursements .... $	4,295,341
Net Change - Assets/Liabilities .... $	(131,300)
Balance on Deposit August 31, 2017 .... $	128,673

INTERNATIONAL EXECUTIVE COMMITTEE GENERAL FUND
Balance on Deposit August 31, 2016 .... $	2,369
Receipts .... $	1,319,780
Disbursements .... $	1,468,269
Net Change - Assets/Liabilities .... $	151,833
Balance on Deposit August 31, 2017 .... $	5,713

LEE UNIVERSITY
Balance on Deposit June 30, 2016 .... $	6,432,907
Receipts .... $	73,837,389
Disbursements .... $	68,755,363
Net Change - Assets/Liabilities .... $	3,891,020
Balance on Deposit June 30, 2017 .... $	7,623,913

MINISTERS WIDOWS FUND
Balance on Deposit August 31, 2016 .... $	253,545
Receipts .... $	129,606
Disbursements .... $	379,650
Net Change - Assets/Liabilities .... $	1
Balance on Deposit August 31, 2017 .... $	3,502

NATIVE AMERICAN MINISTRIES
Balance on Deposit August 31, 2016 .... $	8,677
Receipts .... $	50
Disbursements .... $	—
Net Change - Assets/Liabilities .... $	—
Balance on Deposit August 31, 2017 .... $	8,727

PENIEL FUND RAISING PROJECT
Balance on Deposit August 31, 2016 .... $	15,728
Receipts .... $	5,895
Disbursements .... $	8,336
Net Change - Assets/Liabilities .... $	—
Balance on Deposit August 31, 2017 .... $	13,287

PENTECOSTAL THEOLOGICAL SEMINARY
Balance on Deposit August 31, 2016 .... $	799,202
Receipts .... $	4,606,426
Disbursements .... $	4,549,606
Net Change - Assets/Liabilities.................. $	(286,345)
Balance on Deposit August 31, 2017 .... $	1,142,367

PRISON MINISTRIES
Balance on Deposit August 31, 2016 .... $	4,838
Receipts .... $	219
Disbursements .... $	79
Net Change - Assets/Liabilities.................. $	—
Balance on Deposit August 31, 2017 .... $	4,978

PUBLISHING HOUSE
Balance on Deposit August 31, 2016 .... $	156,337
Receipts .... $	4,404,602
Disbursements .... $	4,501,744
Net Change - Assets/Liabilities.................. $	230,593
Balance on Deposit August 31, 2017 .... $	289,788

WORLD MISSIONS FUND
Balance on Deposit August 31, 2016 .... $	2,660,465
Receipts .... $	26,115,599
Disbursements .... $	24,466,550
Net Change - Assets/Liabilities.................. $	(1,619,704)
Balance on Deposit August 31, 2017 .... $	2,689,810

FINANCIAL REPORT FOR THE YEAR 2017-2018

TITHE FUND —
Balance on Deposit August 31, 2017
Receipts From the Field .... $ 20,040,843
Less Appropriations--
    Aged Ministers .... $ 1,276,947
    Disabled Ministers .... $ 36,495
    IEC General Fund.................. $ 1,278,833
    Ministers Widows.................. $ 23,769
    Total Appropriations .... $ 2,616,044

Net Receipts from the Field .... $ 17,424,799
Other Income .... $ 787,433

Total Net Receipts .... $ 18,212,232
Disbursements .... $ 18,202,704
Net Change — Assets/Liabilities .... $ (8,706)
Balance on Deposit August 31, 2018.................. $ 822

AGED MINISTERS FUND
Balance on Deposit August 31, 2017.................. $ 521,242
Receipts.. $ 1,369,474
Disbursements .... $ 1,698,756
Net Change — Assets/Liabilities .... $ (22,006)
Balance on Deposit August 31, 2018.................. $ 169,954

BENEVOLENCES FUND
Balance on Deposit August 31, 2017.................. $ 83,204
Receipts.. $ 1,046
Disbursements .... $ —
Net Change — Assets/Liabilities .... $ (51,046)
Balance on Deposit August 31, 2018.................. $ 33,204

BUILDING LOAN FUND
Balance on Deposit August 31, 2017.................. $ 2,198
Receipts.. $ —
Disbursements .... $ —
Net Change — Assets/Liabilities .... $ —
Balance on Deposit August 31, 2018.................. $ 2,198

CHURCH PLANTING
Balance on Deposit August 31, 2017.................. $ 241,658
Receipts.. $ 283,786
Disbursements .... $ 215,516
Net Change — Assets/Liabilities .... $ (130,329)
Balance on Deposit August 31, 2018.................. $ 179,599

CMT FUND 61
Balance on Deposit August 31, 2017................... $ 38,363
Receipts.. $ 253,195
Disbursements...................................... $ 233,626
Net Change — Assets/Liabilities .... $ —
Balance on Deposit August 31, 2018................... $ 57,932

CMT FUND 62
Balance on Deposit August 31, 2017................... $ 44,816
Receipts.. $ 224,676
Disbursements...................................... $ 265,260
Net Change — Assets/Liabilities .... $ —
Balance on Deposit August 31, 2018................... $ 4,232

CMT FUND 63
Balance on Deposit August 31, 2017................... $ 59,587
Receipts.. $ 221,600
Disbursements...................................... $ 236,150
Net Change — Assets/Liabilities .... $ —
Balance on Deposit August 31, 2018................... $ 45,037

CMT FUND 64
Balance on Deposit August 31, 2017................... $ 26,908
Receipts.. $ 239,689
Disbursements...................................... $ 263,864
Net Change — Assets/Liabilities .... $ —
Balance on Deposit August 31, 2018................... $ 2,732

CMT — ESCROW
Balance on Deposit August 31, 2017................... $ 12,374
Receipts.. $ 235,333
Disbursements...................................... $ 245,776
Net Change — Assets/Liabilities .... $ —
Balance on Deposit August 31, 2018................... $ 1,931

COMMUNICATIONS FUND
Balance on Deposit August 31, 2017................... $ 3,246
Receipts.. $ 814,611
Disbursements...................................... $ 872,613
Net Change — Assets/Liabilities .... $ (77,416)
Balance on Deposit August 31, 2018................... $ (132,172)

COMPUTER SERVICES
Balance on Deposit August 31, 2017................... $ 2,979
Receipts.. $ 380,329
Disbursements...................................... $ 347,638
Net Change — Assets/Liabilities .... $ —
Balance on Deposit August 31, 2018................... $ 35,670

DISABLED MINISTERS FUND
Balance on Deposit August 31, 2017 .... $	2,037
Receipts .... $	36,495
Disbursements .... $	33,814
Net Change — Assets/Liabilities .... $	—
Balance on Deposit August 31, 2018 .... $	4,718

DISASTER RELIEF FUND
Balance on Deposit August 31, 2017 .... $	84,975
Receipts .... $	769,155
Disbursements .... $	721,970
Net Change — Assets/Liabilities .... $	—
Balance on Deposit August 31, 2018 .... $	132,160

DIVISION OF CARE
Balance on Deposit August 31, 2017 .... $	1,709,538
Receipts .... $	3,680,230
Disbursements .... $	3,644,492
Net Change — Assets/Liabilities .... $	17,893
Balance on Deposit August 31, 2018 .... $	1,763,169

DIVISION OF DISCIPLESHIP
Balance on Deposit August 31, 2017 .... $	249,017
Receipts .... $	4,975,019
Disbursements .... $	5,254,167
Net Change — Assets/Liabilities .... $	47,958
Balance on Deposit August 31, 2018 .... $	17,827

DIVISION OF EDUCATION
Balance on Deposit August 31, 2017 .... $	885,927
Receipts .... $	5,214,505
Disbursements .... $	6,096,067
Net Change — Assets/Liabilities .... $	12,968
Balance on Deposit August 31, 2018 .... $	17,334

DIVISION OF WORLD EVANGELIZATION
Balance on Deposit August 31, 2017 .... $	(2,070)
Receipts .... $	3,053,986
Disbursements .... $	3,058,513
Net Change — Assets/Liabilities .... $	(34,786)
Balance on Deposit August 31, 2018 .... $	(41,383)

GENERAL ASSEMBLY
Balance on Deposit August 31, 2017 .... $	(493,694)
Receipts .... $	1,824,035
Disbursements .... $	2,640,974
Net Change — Assets/Liabilities .... $	(573,176)
Balance on Deposit August 31, 2018 .... $	(1,883,808)

HELPING HANDS
Balance on Deposit August 31, 2017	$	18,399
Receipts	$	86,931
Disbursements	$	230,825
Net Change — Assets/Liabilities	$	172,403
Balance on Deposit August 31, 2018	$	46,908

INSURANCE FUND
Balance on Deposit August 31, 2017	$	128,673
Receipts	$	4,375,714
Disbursements	$	4,350,301
Net Change — Assets/Liabilities	$	(10,941)
Balance on Deposit August 31, 2018	$	143,145

INTERNATIONAL EXECUTIVE COMMITTEE GENERAL FUND
Balance on Deposit August 31, 2017	$	5,713
Receipts	$	1,539,715
Disbursements	$	1,625,924
Net Change — Assets/Liabilities	$	100,000
Balance on Deposit August 31, 2018	$	19,504

LEE UNIVERSITY
Balance on Deposit August 31, 2017	$	7,623,913
Receipts	$	75,752,208
Disbursements	$	73,299,851
Net Change — Assets/Liabilities	$	6,494,195
Balance on Deposit August 31, 2018	$	3,582,075

MINISTERS WIDOWS FUND
Balance on Deposit August 31, 2017	$	3,502
Receipts	$	23,769
Disbursements	$	24,482
Net Change — Assets/Liabilities	$	—
Balance on Deposit August 31, 2018	$	2,789

NATIVE AMERICAN MINISTRIES
Balance on Deposit August 31, 2017	$	8,727
Receipts	$	—
Disbursements	$	—
Net Change — Assets/Liabilities	$	—
Balance on Deposit August 31, 2018	$	8,727

PENIEL FUND RAISING PROJECT
Balance on Deposit August 31, 2017	$	13,287
Receipts	$	6,740
Disbursements	$	4,468
Net Change — Assets/Liabilities	$	—
Balance on Deposit August 31, 2018	$	15,559

PENTECOSTAL THEOLOGICAL SEMINARY
Balance on Deposit August 31, 2017 .... $	1,142,367
Receipts .... $	4,453,993
Disbursements .... $	4,557,900
Net Change — Assets/Liabilities .... $	(38,246)
Balance on Deposit August 31, 2018 .... $	1,076,706

PRISON MINISTRIES
Balance on Deposit August 31, 2017 .... $	4,978
Receipts .... $	6,310
Disbursements .... $	4,789
Net Change — Assets/Liabilities .... $	—
Balance on Deposit August 31, 2018 .... $	6,499

PUBLISHING HOUSE
Balance on Deposit August 31, 2017 .... $	289,788
Receipts .... $	4,576,904
Disbursements .... $	4,528,702
Net Change — Assets/Liabilities .... $	(134,662)
Balance on Deposit August 31, 2018 .... $	203,328

WORLD MISSIONS FUND
Balance on Deposit August 31, 2017 .... $	2,689,810
Receipts .... $	25,630,590
Disbursements .... $	25,608,909
Net Change — Assets/Liabilities .... $	(236,920)
Balance on Deposit August 31, 2018 .... $	2,474,571

Alphabetical
INDEX
to the
2018 *Church of God Book of Discipline,*
Church Order, and Governance

A

Abortion, morally wrong, 31
Addiction and Enslavement, 29
Administrative Bishop, 103 (See State Overseer.)
Affiliation With Church of God, 164
Affiliated Churches, Relation to General Assembly, 165
Affirmation of Our Doctrine, 23
Aged Ministers' Pensioning Plan, 182
  (See Benefits Board, Inc., 178-182.)
Aged Ministers Reformation Sunday Offering, 150
Applicants for Ministry, 96-99
Applicants for Ministry, Divorced and Remarried, 98
Assembly, International General, 65-66
Assembly, International General, Bylaws, 60-61
Assembly, International General, time and place of, 65 (II. 2.)
Assembly, U.S.A. National Council/Assembly, 46, 71 (14.)
Assistant General Overseers, 76 (Executive Bishops, see p. 104.)
Assistant Pastor, 149, 177-178

B

Baptism with (in) the Holy Spirit, 19, 20, 21, 22
Baptism in Water, 19, 21, 31-32
Behavioral Temperance, 28
Benefits Board, Church of God, Inc., 178-182
Bishop, Ordained, Meaning and Usage of Term, 99-102
Bishop: Presiding, Executive, Administrative, 103-104
Bishops, Ordained, Qualifications, Rights and Authorities, 102-104

Boards and Committees, General, 88-90
Borrowing Money, Local Church, 159 (3. A.)
Buying and Building, Local Church, 157-160, 164
Bylaws, Church of God, 59-65
    Amendment of, 64-65
Bylaws, International Executive Council, 63
Bylaws, International General Assembly, 60-61
Bylaws, International General Council, 61-63

C

Care, Ministry of, 85-86
Centennial Resolution, Celebrating Our Heritage (1996), 47-49
Center for Ministerial Care, 86
Chaplains Commission, 87-88
    Board, 87
    Director, 87-88
Child Care, Legal Liability of Local Church, 160-161
Christian Education, Minister of, 106-107
Church—General, 57-59, 52-94
Church of God, Bylaws, 59-65
Church of God Divisional Structure, 52-56
Church of God, Name, 57, 59
Church of God, Vision and Mission, 36-42
Church, Leadership, 44, 142-143
Church—Local, 42, 45, 58, 139-169
Church Members, 141-142, 143-144, 144-147
Church—Local, Development Plan 74, 141
Church, not-for-profit organization, 59 (Article II)
Church and Pastor's Council, 150-151
Church Planting Designated Fund, 80
Church Promotion, 166
Church Property, 156-161
Church Reports, 154-156
Church—State/Regional, 45-46, 126-138

BOOK OF DISCIPLINE, CHURCH ORDER, AND GOVERNANCE

Church and State, Opposed to Union of, 57
Church Treasurer (Local Church), 152-153
Churches, non-Church of God, Affiliation With Church of God, 164-165
Churches or Associations of Churches, Reception of, 59
Clergy, 43
Commitment to Our Pentecostal Heritage, 20
Commitments, Doctrinal, 21-22
   (Doctrinal Affirmation, 23)
Commitments, Practical, 24-31
Communion (The Lord's Supper), 19, 22, 32
Council, Church and Pastor's, 150-151
Council, International, 81-82
Council, International Executive, 63, 68-72
Council of Eighteen, 63, 68
Council, International General, 66-68
Council, State, 130-131
College, Permission to Establish, 91
Compensation for Other Personnel, 177-178
Compensation for Pastors, 174-177
Compensation Scale: Pastor's Minimum, 175-177
Compensation for State Leaders, 172-173
Conferences, Local Church, 147-148
Cost-of-Living Adjustment (to compensation), 175
Construction, Purchase, Remodeling, Local Church, 164
Credentials, International Ministerial, 99
Credentials, Ministerial, 96-108

D

Deacons and Elders in local church, 45, 142-143
Declaration of Faith, 19
Declaration of Faith, Posting, 20
Deeds, Property, Held for Church of God, 156, 158, 164
Deeds, Registration of, 160
Dictatorship in State and Civil Government, Opposed to, 57

Discipleship, Ministry of, (General), 78-79
Discipline of International Executive Committee member, 74-75
Discipline of Members of Church (Exclusion, Appeal), 143, 145-146
Discipline of Offending Ministers, 118-124
Disorderly Ministers [Ministerial Discipline], 111-118
District Overseers, 45, 137
District Youth and Discipleship Director, 138
Divine Healing, 19, 22, 33
Divorce and Remarriage, 32-33
Divorced and Remarried Applicants for Ministry, 98
Doctrinal Commitments, 21-22
   (Doctrinal Affirmation, 23)

E

Editing *Minutes* of International General Assembly, 71 (12. 13.)
Editorial Policies, 94
Elders and Deacons in local church, 45, 142-143
Employment of Family Members by Officials, 172
Euthanasia, morally wrong, 31
Evangel, Church of God, 94
Evangelism and Missions Director (State), 135
Evangelism Program, 135
Evangelistic Associations, 135-136
Example, Spiritual, 24-25
Executive Committee, International, 63, 72-75
Executive Committee Portfolios, of Members, 52-56
Executive Council, International, 63, 68-72
Exhorter, 105-106
Explanatory Notes, 31-34

F

Family Responsibility, 27-28
Family Training Hour (FTH) and/or
   Young Peoples' Endeavor (YPE), 169
Family Worship, 32

Feet Washing, 19, 22, 32
Female Minister, 106
Finance Committee (Local Church), 153-154
Financial System, 153-156
Fraternal Orders, Lodges, 33
   Insurance With, 33, 183

G

Gambling, Stand Against, 143-144
General Assembly, International, 60-61, 65-66
General Assembly, International, time and place of, 65 (II. 2.)
General Board of Education, 90-91
General Board of Trustees, 89-90
General Boards and Committees, 88-90
General Church, 57-59, 51-94
General Council, International, 66-68
General Overseer, 62, 75-76 (Presiding Bishop, see p. 104.)
Government, Church, Centralized Form of, 109-110 (5.), 140-141, 156, 164
Government, Church, Form of, Governing Body Judicial only, 57
Government, Church (General), 51-94
Government, Church (Local), 139-169
Government, Church (Ministry), 95-124
Government, Church (Personnel, USA only), 171-183
Government, Church (State/Regional), 125-138

H

Heritage, Celebrating Our, 47-49
Heritage, Pentecostal, Commitment to Our, 20
Holiness, 19, 21, 34-35
Holiness, Principles of, Resolution, 34-35
Holy Living and Modesty, 29-30, 144
Home, Divine Order in, 28
Home for Children, Canada, 86
Home for Children, Raising Funds for, 86
Homes for Children, Aged, Widows, Ministers, 85 (S14, I., B. 1)

Honorary Ministerial Certificates, 98

I

Incorporation of Local Churches, 58, 162-163
Instructions for Ministers, 109-111
Insurance on Local Property, 160
Insurance, Ministerial and Personnel, 183
Institutions of Higher Education, 91
Integrity, Personal, 26-27
International, Church Is, 46-47
Investments and Loans, 165-166

L

Laity, 41-42
Laity, Procedure for Contacting State Overseer, 149
Laity, Role in International General Assembly, 65-66
Lay Minister Certification, 107-108
Leadership Development, 39
Leadership, 44
Lee University, 91-92
   Board of Directors, 91-92
   President, 92
   Vice President for Business and Finance, 92
Liability of Church for Child Care, Legal, 160-161
Loans and Investments (local church), 165-166
Loans, Local Church Borrowing, 159 (3. A.), 160 (4.)
Local Board of Trustees, 161-162
Local Church, 42, 45, 58, 139-169
Local Church Development Plan, 74, 141
Local Church Leadership (elders and deacons),
   45 (Local Church, 2.), 142-143
Local Church, Relation to General Assembly, 140-141, 143
Local Church and Retired Ministers, 144, 150
Local Church and Unreached People Groups, 84

BOOK OF DISCIPLINE, CHURCH ORDER, AND GOVERNANCE

Lodges, Membership in, 33
   Insurance With, 33, 183
Lord's Supper (Communion), 19, 22, 32
Loyalty to Statements of Faith, 19-20

M

Marriage and Same Sex Relationships, 111
Marriage, Sanctity of, 27-28
Member of Church, Procedure in Dealing With, 146
Member of Church, Right to Appeal, 146-147
Members of Church, 141-144
Members of Church, Exclusion, 143, 145-147
Members of Church, Procedure for Receiving, 141-142
Membership, Associate, Not Permitted, 145
Membership, in Church, 141
Membership Roll To Be Maintained, 145
Membership, Transfer, 144-145
Military Service, Combatant, 33
Minister (See Ordained Bishop, Ordained Minister, Female Minister, Minister of Music, Minister of Christian Education, Exhorter, Lay Minister.)
Minister, Disorderly, [Ministerial Discipline], 111-118
Minister, Offending, [Ministerial Discipline], 118-124
Minister, Offending, Appeals, 88, 123-124
Minister of Christian Education, 106-107
Minister of Music, 106-107
Ministerial Care, Center for, 86
Ministerial Certificates, Honorary, 98
Ministerial Credentials, 96-108
Ministerial Credentials, International, 99
Ministerial Development, State Board, 133-134
Ministerial Discipline, 111-118, 118-124
Ministerial Internship Program, 96
Ministerial Reporting, 108-109

Ministers, Instructions for, 109-111
Ministers' Retirement Plan (Benefits Board, Inc.), 178-182
Ministry of Care, 85-86
Ministry, Scriptural Principles for, 35-36
Minutes (*Church of God Book of Discipline, Church Order, and Governance*),
    local church to provide treasurer with current copy, 152 (I. 3.)
Minutes, Editing by International Executive Council, 71 (12. 13.)
Missions (Ministry of USA Missions) 79-80
    Board, 79
    Resolution on USA Missions, 79
    Church Planting Designated Fund, 80
Missions (Ministry of World Missions), 80-84
    Board, 80
    International Council, 81-82
    Director, 82-83
    Assistant Director, 83
Missions Funds, Methods Used for Raising, 83-84
Modest Appearance and Holy Living, 29-30, 144
Moral Purity, 25-26
Music, Minister of, 106-107
Music, State Board, 136-137

N

Name of Church, 57, 59
National Assembly, 46, 71 (14.)
National Council/Assembly for U.S.A., 46
    Structure and Time for, 71 (14.)
New Birth (Regeneration), 19, 21, 31

O

Obligation, Social, 30-31
Offending Ministers [Ministerial Discipline], 118-124
Ordained Bishop, 99-104
Ordained Bishop, Meaning and Usage of Term Bishop, 99-102

Ordained Minister, 104-105
Ordinances of Church:
   (Water Baptism, Lord's Supper, Feet Washing), 19, 21-22, 31, 32
Organization Report (1994), 45-47
Overseer, Assistant to General, 76 (Executive Bishop, see p. 104.)
Overseer, District, 45, 137
Overseer, General, 75-76 (Presiding Bishop, see p. 104.)
Overseer, State, 124-127 (Administrative Bishop, see p. 103.)
Overseer, State, Appointed by
   International Executive Committee, 73 (S6. III. 1.), 126
Overseer, State,
   Procedure for laity contacting, 149

P

Pastor, 148-150
Pastor, Appointed by State Overseer, 148
Pastor, Assistant, 149, 177-178
Pastor, To Receive Reformation Sunday Offering
   for Aged Ministers, 150
Pastor's Compensation, 174-175
   Minimum Compensation Scale, 175-177
Pastor's Council (Local Church), 150-151
Pastor's Sabbatical, 177
Pastoral Change, Procedure for Effecting, 149
Pastoral Preference Expression, 149
Pathway Press, Name, 94
Pentecostal Heritage, Commitment to Our, 20
Pentecostal Worship, 37
Pensioning Plan for Aged Ministers, 182-183, (see 175, IV.)
   (Also see Retirement Plan, Benefits Board, Inc., 178-182.)
Personal Integrity, 26-27
Porfolios of Executive Committee Members, 52-56
Posting Declaration of Faith, 20
Practical Commitments, 24-31

Presiding Bishop, 104 (See General Overseer.)
Previous Notice, To Amend Bylaws of Church of God, 64-65
Property, All Held for Church of God, 158, 164
Property, Church, 156-161
Publications, Ministry of, 93-94
Purity, Moral, 25-26

R

Reformation Sunday Offering for Aged Ministers, 150
Reports (Local Church), 154-156
Reports, Monthly, by local church treasurer, 153 (III. 6.)
    Percentage of Tithes to be sent to
    International and State/Regional Offices, 154
Reporting, Ministerial, 108-109
Retired Ministers and Local Church, 144
Retirement Plan for Aged Ministers, 182-183
    Church of God Benefits Board, Inc., 178-182
    Supplemental Retirement Benefit Program, 175 (IV.)

S

Sabbatical for Pastors, 177
Salaries (See Compensation.)
Sanctification, 19, 21
Sanctity of Life, Protecting, 31
Sanctity of Marriage, 27-28, (also see 111)
Scriptural Principles for Ministry, 35-36
Secretary General, 77 (Executive Bishop, see p. 104.)
Social Obligation, 30-31
Spiritual Example, 24-25
State Board of Ministerial Development, 133-134
State Board of Trustees, 131-133
State and Church, Opposed to Union of, 57
State Council, 130-131
State Evangelism and Missions Director, 135

Statements of Faith, Loyalty to, 19-20
State Music Board, 136
State Overseers, 126-130 (Administrative Bishops, see p. 103.)
State World Missions Board, 136
State Youth and Discipleship Board, 134
State Youth and Discipleship Director, 134-135
Sunday School, 168-169
Supplemental Retirement Benefit Program, 175 (IV.)

T

Teachings of Church of God, 20-21
   Declaration of Faith, 19
   Doctrinal Commitments, 21-22
   Practical Commitments, 24-31
Temperance, Behavioral, 28-29
Tithing, 22, (Q and A, 34), 154
Tithes, Percentage to be sent to International
   and State/Regional Offices, 154
Tobacco, Against Use of, (Addiction and Enslavement, 29), 33 (VIII)
Tongues, Speaking with other, 19 (8. 9.), 20, 21-22 (9.)
Transfer of Membership, 144-145
Treasurer, Local Church, 152-153
Treasurer to be provided a copy of the current book of *Minutes*
   (*Church of God Book of Discipline, Church Order,*
   and Governance), 152 (I. 3.)
Trustees, General Board, 89-90
Trustees, Local Board, 161-162
Trustees, State Board, 131-133

U

United States of America National Council/Assembly, 46, 71 (14.)
Unreached People Groups and Local Church, 84 (VI.)

USA Missions, Ministry of, 79-80
    Board, 79
    Resolution on USA Missions, 79
    Church Planting Designated Fund, 80

V

Vacancies, Filling:
    Assistant General Overseers, 76
    Council of Eighteen, 69
    Elected General Ministry Leader, 85
    General Overseer, 76
    International Executive Committee, Two or More Members, 72
    Secretary General, 77
Vision and Mission of Church, 36
    Commitments to, 37-42, 42-47

W

Water Baptism, 19, 21, 31-32
Women's Ministries (Local Church) [Women's Discipleship], 166-168

Women's Ministries (State) [Women's Discipleship], 138

World Missions, Ministry of, 80-84
    Board, 80-81
    International Council, 81-82
    Director, 82-83
    Assistant Director, 83
World Missions Board (State), 136
World Missions Funds, Methods Used for Raising, 83-84
Worship, Family, 32
Worship, Pentecostal, 37

Y

Youth and Discipleship, State Board, 134

Youth and Discipleship, Ministry of, (General), 78-79
   Director, 78
   Assistant Director, 78-79
Youth and Discipleship, State Director, 134-135
Youth and Discipleship, District Director, 138
YPE (Young People's Endeavor), 169

NOTES

NOTES

NOTES

NOTES